"*Why Customers Leave* will become the new first reading for all members of my team, mandatory next reading for those already with us, and our top recommendation to all of our clients."

—Brian Smith, PhD, senior partner,
IA Business Advisors

"David Avrin says, 'You are not going to like everything I have to say in this book.' Avrin's right. But you're not looking for happy hoohah. You're looking for actionable insights that will improve your business. Read his book. You'll thank me later."

—Bruce Turkel, author of *All About Them*

"David Avrin makes a powerful case for Customer Experience as the only sustainable competitive advantage. In his engaging and provocative new book, *Why Customers Leave*, Avrin reveals a wide range of company behaviors that alienate customers, frustrate prospects, and drive both into the arms of your competition. Learn what you must do, and what you must avoid. Buy this book to see yourself as your customers see you."

—Ron Kaufman, *New York Times* bestselling
author of *Uplifting Service*

Foreword by *New York Times* bestselling author
LARRY WINGET

WHY CUSTOMERS LEAVE

(AND HOW TO WIN THEM BACK)

DAVID AVRIN

**CAREER
PRESS**

This edition first published in 2019 by Career Press, an imprint of
Red Wheel/Weiser, LLC
With offices at:
65 Parker Street, Suite 7
Newburyport, MA 01950
www.redwheelweiser.com

ISBN: 978-1-63265-151-8
Library of Congress Cataloging-in-Publication Data
available upon request.

Cover design by Kathryn Sky-Peck
Interior by Lauren Manoy
Typeset in Minion Pro and Cabin

Printed in the United States of America
LB
10 9 8 7 6 5 4 3 2 1

DEDICATION

*To Tiffany Lauer, my brilliant assistant and business manager,
who delivers the consummate customer
experience for our clients every day.*

CONTENTS

Acknowledgments...ix

Foreword..xiii

Preface:
  Don't Skip This...xvii

Introduction:
  Blink and They're Gone..1

1 Stop Telling Us No..11

2 Don't Fake It Until You Make It...22

3 Automation Kills Loyalty..30

4 Don't Close–Ever..38

5 Don't Be Hard to Reach..46

6 Don't Pee on My Leg and Tell Me It's Raining......................................55

7 We Don't Want to Do Business Your Way...63

8 Don't Punish Everyone for the Actions of a Few....................................73

9 Fix Your Dysfunctional Website..82

10 You Get One Chance, So Don't Blow It......................... 91

11 It's Not What You Want to Say, It's What We Want
    to Hear.. 100

12 My Call Is Not Very Important to You 109

13 Don't Treat Me Like You Want to Be Treated 116

14 Don't Pass the Buck (and Don't Throw Coworkers
    Under the Bus)..124

15 Stop Making Us Do Your Work.....................................132

16 Your Stalking Is Creeping Us Out................................ 140

17 Avoid the Sin of Omission 148

18 Your Management Fails to Manage............................155

19 Show Us That You Care About Your Business 164

20 Stop Wasting Our Time 170

21 Stop Being Cheap..175

22 Don't Take Us for Granted.. 181

23 Being Good Is No Longer Good Enough.....................187

Afterword:
    Be a Great Customer 191

Notes...193

Index...195

ACKNOWLEDGMENTS

When Allison Janney won the Oscar for Best Supporting Actress for her role in the movie *I, Tonya,* she famously walked to the microphone to give her acceptance speech, looked at the audience, and said: "I did it all by myself." And then she smiled and said: "Nothing further from the truth." So it is with writing a book.

The thanks don't merely go to those who surround the process of writing, or the patience from those who surrounding the writer himself (in this case), but to those encountered during all the years when the knowledge was gained, the opinions were formed, and the wisdom was honed.

I'd like to thank all those who provided both stellar and horrific business experiences throughout my life. It is your diligence or ineptitude, your attentiveness or indifference, that formed the basis for the stories and lessons shared in this book.

To the influential people in my life:

A big thanks to my brilliant literary agent, Jill Marsal of the Marsal Lyon Literary Agency. I so appreciate your grounding wisdom when I have my head in the clouds (or up my ass). Thanks for your effective advocacy and sage counsel.

Thank you to Michael Pye from Career Press for taking a chance on yet another book and for believing in this project and putting your resources behind it. I will make you proud.

To my amazing, hardworking, diligent, and very loyal assistant and business manager, Tiffany Lauer: approaching seven years working together, I would not be where I am without your feedback, wisdom, support, prodding, and partnership in this business. You are family.

To the group chairs and members of Vistage International, the world's leading chief executive organization. It is due in large part to the more than 4,000 one-on-one conversations I have had with company leaders over the past decade that I am better equipped to teach, share, cajole, and mentor. I feel that I have learned as much as I have taught.

To those who have given me feedback on this book: My awesome brother, Doug Avrin, you are wise, honest, and the most loving man I know. If any one of you has ever received a t-shirt or coffee mug that says "World's Greatest Dad," just know that it doesn't belong to you. You are only borrowing it from my brother Doug. Give it back to him when you are done.

To the brilliant and generous John DiJulius of the DiJulius Group: Many will speak or write on customer experience, but John lives it, teaches it, models it, and bleeds it through his pores. You are the real deal, brother.

To the six-time *New York Times* bestselling author, media celebrity, teller-of-truths, Hall of Fame Speaker, and all-around real man, Larry Winget: I am humbled by your kindness and validating words, your phenomenal foreword to this book, and for modeling what authenticity and integrity are on stage, in business, and in life. Larry is among the most captivating, relevant, and actionable speakers in the world. Look him up!

To my tribe at the National Speakers Association: Few people understand better than you do, the adrenaline rush of a thousand audience members on their feet and the ego boost of a book signing, only to be followed by a lonely chicken dinner and Uber ride to the airport. You are my family and my brothers- and sisters-in-arms. See you on the road.

To my precious children, who are no longer children, Sierra, Sydney, and Spencer: my role as speaker, consultant, coach, and author pale in comparison to my most important role as your dad. It has been my greatest joy to watch you grow into powerful, generous, and loving people. You inspire me every day. I was going to say that you have no idea how proud I am of all of you, but actually, you do know.

To my new kids, Hunter and Will, who are not kids either: I am excited and proud to be in your life (and crazy in love with your mom)!

And to my angel, Laurel: Your love, support, patience, humor, wisdom, and constant encouragement astonishes me every day. Knowing that you will be by my side for all my days gives me fuel to take on anything. I adore you.

Finally, to the thousands of supporters who have been in my audience, received my newsletter, connected with me on social media, commented on my Facebook posts, retweeted my irreverence to the masses, and supported me through the years—a very big thank you! Your support means the world to me and my family.

FOREWORD

I've said for years that being in business would be great if it weren't for employees and customers. Think about it: Employees and customers are the source of nearly every problem you have. Employees have a tendency to forget they are there to make the business profitable by serving customers well and making them happy, which is what keeps them coming back. After all, happy customers who share their money with you is what keeps those employees paid, and they should realize that. But when that most basic aspect of a business relationship breaks down, that's a problem—a big, costly problem.

And customers . . . wow! They want and expect so much these days. But why shouldn't they? They have so many options. There's you, there's the guy down the street, and the thousands of other businesses that are just a click or two away. The obvious truth is that you aren't the only game in town. You are just one more on a long list of businesses where they can get what you have to offer possibly quicker, probably cheaper, and maybe from someone who values their business more and demonstrates it in a variety of ways.

As for the Internet, I would much rather buy with a click and have it in on my doorstep in a couple of days and never have to talk to an unknowledgeable, surly employee who is more interested looking at Instagram than they are in me, my needs, desires, problems, and money. Wouldn't you?

Those are the issues almost every business deals with almost every day in some way. Your employees and your customers hold the success of your company in their hands. But you know that. How could you not?

So why is that you know it and are still dealing with all of the problems (and maybe even more) that I just described? It's not for lack of knowledge as there is plenty of that around. It's usually for lack of implementation. I have been doling out business, personal, financial, and parenting advice for a lot of years.

After having given thousands of speeches and selling millions of books, I have discovered people don't do much of anything with the knowledge they have at their fingertips. There are lots of reasons for that, but I think one of the big ones is that most of the information is so abstract it ends up being confusing. Or it is just the opposite and is so specific that people can't understand how to apply it to their particular situation.

Good news: This book isn't like that. It is logical, practical, easily implementable, and well, it just makes sense! I like that. I read it and found myself nodding my head up and down saying, "Yep, I get it. He's right. I need to take action on that right now." You will be the same way.

So when you find your customers leaving and aren't sure exactly what to do to stop the drain or to get them back, what do you do? Do you fire everyone who doesn't treat the customer right and start over? That's a possibility for sure, but not a very smart one. Do you trash your competition in order to build yourself up in the eyes of the customer? That's a short game you will never ultimately win. Do you out-advertise them? Someone else can always spend more money.

Most people when faced with a problem, any problem, start looking at how to solve their problem. Of course, right? That's exactly what they should do! Well, not necessarily. Figuring out what to do and how to do it is indeed important, but probably not the first step. That's what I like about this book. David Avrin will give you the how and what, but he starts with why. I like that. A lot.

Too many folks jump right into how and what and get really busy with fixing the problem, only to find out after much effort, time, and possibly expense that the problem isn't fixed at all. That can be a frustrating, even maddening, experience. But it's because they never figured out *why* they have the problem. David wants you to think about why you do what you do and realize why your customers react and respond the way they do. In other words, "Why am I in this mess?" That sounds simple, and although it is, it's really powerful. It's powerful because it will make you think. Thinking is always hard, and thinking about how dumb we sometimes are is even harder.

Here is another reason I like this book: David gives you a better approach to doing business so your customer will never leave you. He doesn't say this is the only approach or the best approach (even though it probably is the best approach). He just shows you what you are probably doing wrong and then suggests a better approach. I like the lack of arrogance in this. I am tired of authors and speakers saying this is *the* way to do things. I have discovered there are as many ways to be successful as there are successful people. I know better than to believe there is only one way. David does too. These better approaches are a gift to you. In fact, they are a huge gift that when used, can save your business.

Here's my favorite thing about the book: It is grounded to core values. If you know anything about who I am and what I do for a living, you know how important that is to me. Honesty, integrity, kindness, gratitude, courtesy, and work ethic are values that we all see collapsing around us. David grounds this work in those values. That makes me proud to put my name on it and proud he asked me to write this foreword.

So, here's what I suggest: Open your mind, be coachable to better ideas, ask yourself the questions he asks of you, be honest with yourself with the answers, then buy every single member of your team this book and use it for discussion and training. Doing those things stacks the deck in your favor better than you will ever imagine.

Now, turn the page and start taking your business to the next level.

—Larry Winget
Six-time *New York Times* and *Wall Street Journal*
bestselling author, Hall of Fame Speaker,
social commentator, and TV personality

Preface:
Don't Skip This

Okay, lets get this out of the way: You are not going to like everything I have to say in this book, but it's important that you listen. To be honest, *I* don't like everything I say in this book, but I believe every word of it. I do promise that you will recognize the problems and behaviors that I detail in the pages to follow, and most will resonate. Some will make you nod your head in agreement, and others will make you throw up you hands in disgust. Others will even make you smile a bit. As a consumer, you've been there. Hell, you are there! As a business owner or leader, you may need a wake-up call. This book is that wake-up call.

In this book, I'm going to tell you what you need to hear because it will save you money and it will even make you money. It may even help you become a better person. Right now, in some ways, your behavior—some behavior—is costing you money and relationships. Your cost-cutting is costing you customers, and your policies, designed to make life easier and more efficient for your employees, are driving clients and customers away.

Here is the uncomfortable truth: As good as you are, most prospective customers don't choose you. They choose someone else. Unless you have more than a 50 percent market share (rare), most of your prospects choose to do business with your competitors instead of you. Why? This book will help you uncover or discover some of those reasons.

And although I speak for a living, I'm not a motivational speaker. As a business author, I'm not your cheerleader, parent, teacher, or therapist who is here to pump you up and tell you how brilliant you are. I am not your personal coach or accountability partner. I am something far more important. *I am your customer.* I am your client, patient, or vendor. Better still, I am your prospective customer or client. I'm the one deciding whether to do business with you, and I have so many choices. You are merely one of them.

As your customer, if you make me wait, I get frustrated. If you tell me no, I will easily find someone who will tell me yes. If you can't make me happy, meet my needs, and give me a good experience, I will find someone who can and will. It's not a big deal. I do it every day. Then again, so do you.

In this book, we are going to question why you conduct your business the way you do. We will look at how you design your customer interactions, tell you which ones they/we don't like, and explain why we leave you for your competitors. Sometimes you will agree with me, and sometimes you won't. It's okay. You won't hurt my feelings. I don't always agree with you either, but we can still listen and consider.

We are going to talk a bit about yesteryear—the way things used to be. Not simply to wax nostalgic about a simpler time, but to provide perspective and context. I am going to contrast how and why our lives are the way they are compared to the way things used to be, and how these new dynamics are driving the opinions we have, the behaviors we engage in, and the decisions we make.

To be clear, this will *not* be an academic exploration of demographic trends, economic theory, behavioral drivers, and generational shifts. Not only is that not the book I want to write, it's not the book I want to read.

Plain and simple, this book is a rant. This book is a real-world reflection of what your customers think and how they feel about doing business with you. Lest you think this is simply an exercise in catharsis, know that there is a method to the madness and a structure to the lessons.

Other books might explore creative ways to bolster your customer experience and thrill your customers, but I believe that fixing the problems you may be unaware of is a crucial first step and foundation that every successful business is built upon.

Also, I will warn you in advance that I write more for the ear than for the page. I write like I speak. And if it bothers you that I start sentences with "And" or "But," then you'll just need to get over that. But that is up to you.

Each chapter of this book will be structured in this way:

The background

Examples of the customer-repelling behavior

Why you do it

Why we hate it

A better approach

My job is to highlight a pain that you may be unaware of, stretch open that wound, pour some salt on it, and offer the medicine you need.

Keep in mind that not everything covered in this book will apply to your specific business model. Turn a page or two, and something else will. It is the nature of a book like this that different scenarios will resonate with different business models. Don't let a few near-misses lull you into a dismissive posture. More hits will come in the pages to follow. And although every scenario may not apply to your specific business, I am confident that the vast majority of scenarios will surely resonate!

Finally, this book is intentionally structured to be taken in small doses. You are welcome to devour it in a few marathon sessions, but it was designed for you to absorb a thoughtful lesson or two, share a discussion with your team, and never feel like you had to stop in the middle of a chapter. The chapters are simply not that long. Put it on your desk, on your bedroom nightstand, or leave it in your bathroom. Just pick it up from time to time.

And as I say with all the books I write: Ignore what your teachers taught you in school and write all over this book. Highlight passages, dog-ear the pages, and write in the margins. It's your book! It's not a novel, for crying out loud. It's a business book and meant to be analyzed, discussed with your team, and acted upon. Better still, if something resonates, tweet it out! @DavidAvrin

So go make yourself a cup of coffee. Then, stop by your bathroom, grab a hand mirror, and lay it on the table next to you. You're going to need to pick it up more often than you'd like.

Let's begin.

Introduction:
Blink and They're Gone

We often miss opportunity because it's
dressed in overalls and looks like work.
–Thomas A. Edison

I walked into a big box electronic store on a Wednesday evening looking for a new, high-end camera. I have a video recording studio with a big white screen backdrop in my office where I record short marketing and customer experience videos to post online. After using my iPhone for years to record, I realized that it was time for an upgrade. So I walked to the camera section in the back of the store and began to explore. After about fifteen minutes of perusing and handling all of the different models, I found the exact camera that I was looking for. A little pricey, but it was perfect! It had the manual aperture adjustments that I need and an extra microphone input.

So here is the question: Did I buy that camera, yes or no? No! I pulled my cell phone out of my pocket, found the exact same item online for $87 cheaper, and I clicked to buy it as I walked out of the store.

I searched through Craigslist.org trying to find someone to fix a few broken sprinkler heads in my yard. I said that I was going to fix them for months, but I never got around to it. So I decided to just bite the bullet and hire someone who knows what they're doing. I typed in the search criteria, and Craigslist delivered a reasonably long list of sprinkler repair guys in my part of town. But when I called the first one, I got an answering machine that said:

"Thanks for calling XYZ Sprinkler Install and Repair. We are out of the office right now. Leave a message, and we will call you when we get back."

So . . . did I leave a message? No! I just called the next one on the list, and the next one, until someone answered, and that's who I hired. Nobody leaves messages!

My sweetheart and I were going out to dinner on a Friday night. Our kids were out at a high school football game, and we had a rare "date night" out alone! We wanted to try a new Thai restaurant, and I thought this would be a perfect time to go. So I went online to make a reservation but decided to check a few user reviews to be safe. As I scrolled down, I saw a plethora of positive reviews, but I noticed several comments from recent weeks that were less than flattering.

So, once again, did I make a reservation? No! We don't get a date night often enough. We opt to head to a familiar restaurant that we already know and like instead. There is no reason to take a chance on something that may not be great.

What do all of these scenarios have in common? They are all examples of sales that never happened. They are customers who were lost, prospects who got away, and lookey-loos who stopped looking.

The most painful truth in your business is this: Your biggest source of lost revenue are the prospects you never knew about. They drove by, but they didn't stop in. They called, but hung up before you answered the phone. They dropped by your business, but they turned around and left before they were engaged, or they visited your website and clicked away without buying anything or leaving their contact information. And the worst part about this is that you have no idea who those people were, or how many of them there were!

We live in an amazing but challenging time. The choices are vast and the quality of providers is high. We have more choices than ever before, and most of those choices are great ones. Be clear: You are not the only good choice. Your prospects have countless choices—including the choice to not buy at all!

Moreover, we are bombarded by messages telling us that we don't need you. We don't need to pay the 6 percent real estate commission. We don't need to buy a traditional mattress in a store. We can buy a car without the car salesperson, and we don't need to wait around hoping that you will call us back.

We can't take for granted the fact that customers will always need us. They won't. They can buy from anybody or nobody. Every day, I see great companies who work hard to create quality products and services, build strong internal teams, take on huge financial risks for their families, spend significant dollars to attract new customers, and then blow it by dropping the ball when it matters most. You have customers right where you want them—on the phone, in your store, at your office, on your website—and then you frustrate them in some way.

The unfortunate truth is that most of them (and you) don't realize that you're doing it. Don't tell me that my call is very important to you and then place me on hold for forty minutes! You hate that as a consumer, so why do you think your customers will be okay with it? They aren't!

You might be tempted to dismiss much of what I will talk about as "first-world problems." Resist that urge. Just because there are people starving in an impoverished nation or living each day in a war-torn region who would love to have our lives and our challenges, doesn't negate the fact that a problem in the mind of your prospect is still a problem. Annoyed prospects are customers on the way out the door, taking their first-world problems and their money with them.

Occasionally, I will post a challenging customer experience scenario on my social media pages for my audience to consider, only to get the inevitable dismissive response that my complaint is a petty "first-world problem." Perhaps, but the offending company just lost my business. Do you think the loss of my future revenue, and that of my family and those I tell, is a petty issue for them? Quite to the contrary. Lost customers and lost revenue is a huge issue for business—wherever in the world you may be.

The fact is that we all get frustrated by how we are treated by companies. In yesteryear, we would tell a close circle of friends, or just mutter our frustration to ourselves. We live in a different world today. Virtually everyone shares—everything!

For crying out loud, millions of people share pictures of the food they're eating.

This new "oversharing" dynamic has become an over-sharing culture. What was once an anomaly and dismissed as a behavior of young teens has become pervasive in our society. I am just as guilty, or just as compliant, however you want to look at it. Why is this important? Because in our society, we "out" underperformers. We share our bad experiences constantly!

We all grew up in a business world with the well-worn, and universally accepted maxim that the average customer with a positive experience will tell two or three people, and those with a negative experience will tell ten. The notion is never really questioned and often repeated in some similar fashion. It fits with conventional wisdom.

My friends, none of that is true anymore! Today, when there is a negative experience we don't tell ten people. Now, we tell thousands. Sometimes, we tell millions! Don't agree? Just try dragging a paying customer off your airline and see how far that spreads. Or suffocate a puppy in the overhead bin. Or arrest gentlemen in your Starbucks because they didn't buy coffee and wanted to use the restroom. Or video-tape racist or homophobic "skits" at you college fraternity. I'm not trying to be funny. It's tragic, offensive, and perfect fodder for social media sharing and sharing and sharing.

In yesteryear, we did everything we could to placate dis-satisfied customers. We would work with them and try to solve their problems. At some point however, we might have to accept the fact that they are never going to be happy, and we have to write them off. We can't write anyone off any-more. We need to be very concerned about everyone who is dissatisfied with their experience, and not just for that potential lost business, but for all those they will tell, both directly and indirectly. Because that negative information or review posted online doesn't go away—*ever!*

I ask my kids, "Do you know the difference between love and the Internet? Answer: The Internet is forever . . . and ever!" I know. That's a terribly cynical thing to say to young people, but the point is important. The permanence of embarrassing situations, negative comments, and reviews is profoundly impactful on your business. The good and bad news is that your competitors face the same challenge. The world has changed.

Reputation management companies have sprung up just to help companies deal with negative content posted online about their businesses. They charge a healthy fee to post positive content in order to push the less-flattering posts further down and off the first page.

You should fully expect that any negative experience with your business, at any organizational level, will be shared. If it's not, then you dodged a bullet. But are you willing to take that risk?

I'm not talking about your customer service. At the bare minimum, you should be holding your people accountable to provide good, courteous service. We are going to assume that you know the importance of basic service and the dignity of your customers. We are going to assume that you have strong training and consistent oversight of your team to ensure that your people deliver and meet the needs of your customers. If you fail at this basic level, then you are not yet ready to tackle the behavior discussed in this book.

And to be clear, this book is not permission to provide subpar products and services and simply mask those with a strong customer experience. No, folks. We are not here to put lipstick on a pig.

"Customer service" is an individual's behavior at the point of customer contact. "Customer experience," by contrast, is your organizational policies and behaviors, and how your value proposition is delivered. It is how you design your customer interface at every point of contact. How do prospects find you, reach you, engage with you, buy from you? How do they get their questions answered, their products or services delivered, and concerns addressed? And while customer service is certainly an important part of that delivery, your intentional policies, procedures, and oversight will drive those interactions.

Your biggest problem, and the chief source of your lost prospects and revenue, is not your customer service. It's your ingrained beliefs and desire for operational efficiency, cost savings, and predictability of employee behavior that are driving your customers to your competitors. You can blame Amazon or online alternatives all you want for decreased sales, but it is you, and only you, who has the responsibility to fix what is less than ideal in your customers' path and make it better than the cheaper alternatives. Are you going to roll over, or are you going to fight for your business?

In this book, I am going to ask "Why?" a lot. Why do you say no? Why do you make it hard to reach you? Why do you email me without permission? Why do you survey me constantly? Why do you treat me like a shoplifter and check my receipt as I leave your store? Why do you keep me on hold? Why do you automate your response? Why do you quote your inflexible policies, make me do your job, mislead me, fail to provide basics that your competitors have adopted, make me click through endless website links, or navigate your voicemail prompts? These are not rhetorical questions. I want to know why.

And while not everything covered in the following chapters will apply to you in your business, virtually everything discussed affects you as a consumer. You will recognize the scenarios and maddening company behaviors. Like you, I am sick of being ignored, taken for granted, or being told no.

This book is about your reputation. What are you known for in the marketplace? And is your reputation—your brand—being derailed without you recognizing it? Your brand promise is who you say you are, but your customer experience is how you deliver it.

In this book, I will detail twenty-three ways that companies' policies, procedures, and practices drive us away to alternatives. They are relayed and explained in no particular order. There are, no doubt, countless other reasons, but twenty-three felt like a good number. Perhaps feedback in the months to follow will form the basis of another book. Any attempt to put the chapters in an order of importance, frequency, or pervasiveness would be too subjective. Let's tackle them as they come. Just try to resist the urge to be dismissive or defensive.

There are three central themes that you will recognize being revisited throughout this book. These three key consumer mindsets often occur simultaneously and typify today's profoundly different consumer. Most notably, they illustrate how expectations have changed in significant ways in a very short period of time. (Remember, the iPhone was released just over ten years ago.) These three shifts are the primary themes I share with audiences in my speaking and with organizations in my consulting. They are the core reasons that heeding the lessons of this book are so crucial if you want to be competitive in business today and survive for tomorrow.

Immediacy: We have always desired instant gratification, but it is only today's world that we have come to expect it. We want immediate answers to our questions, online access to product information, turn-by-turn directions to our meeting, real-time conversations at 35,000 feet, and the ability to buy with just one click.

Today, we don't leave voicemail messages for prospective service providers who are out of the office, we just move on to another. We won't jump through your hoops to get access to your hidden prices; we'll find someone who will tell us their price right away without playing games. And if someone doesn't respond to our text message within a minute or two, we feel personally slighted. Plain and simple, those who make us wait will too often lose the business to competitors who don't.

Individuality: You can substitute the words "flexible" or "customizable" if you wish.

We don't want to do business your way, we want it our way. A one-size-fits-all approach is for your benefit—not ours. We want gluten-free options, the ability to make menu substitutions, the flexibility to work from home, the ability to customize our pair of Converse All-Stars online with the colors and patterns of our choosing, the option for same-day delivery (even if it costs more), and to not be restricted by your office hours.

As kids, we hurried to choose our favorite token when we played Monopoly. Today, kids not only choose their own character in their video games, but they also choose their clothes, hair, vehicles, weapons, and more. Others let us customize our experience today, and you need to find way to be flexible as well.

Humanity: Finally, lest you think I am going to wax philosophical about the importance of being a good corporate citizen or using sustainable environmental practices—I'm not. It's for you decide what is important to you and your organization. Many customers care; others don't. I'm talking about humanity as it pertains to us—your customers and clients. We want to know that our unique circumstances, needs, wants and requests matter.

Too often, in an effort to create streamlined processes, achieve greater consistency in policies, and even a measure of predictability in our interactions and revenue, we neuter our employees in the process. We are so worried that they will make a bad decision that we don't let them make any decisions.

Too many companies have relegated their people to simply quoting policies instead of solving problems. When someone asks for a reasonable accommodation because of an unforeseen circumstance, our employees say, "Sorry. We can't allow that."

People want to feel as if their requests are being truly heard and not being met with robotic responses—from real live people. You'll hear me talking throughout about the importance of guidelines instead of policies and reasonable flexibility to help real people with real needs.

1

STOP TELLING US NO

Those who deny freedom to others,
deserve it not for themselves.
–Abraham Lincoln

Psychologists tell us that the most offensive word to the human ear is "no." (If you ask my teenage daughter, she will tell you that word is "moist." But I digress.) Not surprisingly, the visceral reaction to "no" transcends language and cultural boundaries. Whether it's no, or *nyet, nien,* or *non,* we don't like to be told that we can't have what we want. Conversely, "no" is also considered the most powerful word as it can help us set boundaries, decline participation in harmful activities, avoid overburdening our schedules, protect our physical space, and prevent onions from making their way onto our burgers.

So as we look to generate sales and earn revenue from paying customers, why do we say no so often? This isn't about the appropriate response to informative yes-or-no questions. Often, "no" is simply a response to a circumstance rather than a rejection of a request.

"Is there a Chinese restaurant on this block?"

"Sorry, no. But we have a great Indian restaurant next door."

I'm talking about declining a request from a customer or client, falling back on company policy, or failing to offer a requested amenity. (Like outlets for charging cell phones.)

Now, to be clear, we have softer ways of saying no. We say things like, "Oh, I'm sorry, but we don't allow that." Or, "Gee, I would like to, but we won't be able to accommodate you." However you and your team couch it, you are telling us we can't have—or even pay for—what we want.

This isn't an issue of the customer always being right. This is an issue of accommodation and retention. It isn't about merely doing the right thing because it's the right thing to do, although that should be our fallback position. This is about profit and loyalty.

Lest you immediately jump in your mind to the things that you simply cannot do in your business, trust me. I get it. There are things that will never make sense in business. Every project can't be custom from scratch. Schedule changes that affect your entire team and take you off other client work often can't be accommodated, and your business has to remain profitable. What I am referring to is all the other times when a simple accommodation would be little skin off your nose, but would save a sale, please a customer, and foster loyalty.

"But that's a slippery slope!" you say. "If we start allowing everyone to substitute a menu item, then everyone will do it."

Nope. Not buying it. Bogus argument. "Everyone" isn't at the table when you agree to substitute shrimp for chicken. You don't find a way to say yes because you don't want to. You don't do it because you don't want your cooks in the kitchen complaining about special orders. You don't do it because you don't know how much extra to charge and don't want to take the time to figure it out.

But you know what? The lady would rather have shrimp! So give her shrimp and charge an extra couple bucks! You just made more money. She is pleased and will not only give you her future business but will likely tell others of her great experience! What's the other option? *Not* giving her what she asked for? So she leaves unhappy, doesn't come back, posts a negative Yelp review, and tells all of her 5,000 Facebook friends what a crappy place this is? Saying no when you could easily say yes—to a paying customer—is both stupid and lazy.

I stopped by the hotel front desk at 7:00 a.m. on the way out to a speaking gig. "Good morning," I say. "I'm going to need a late checkout, please."

"I'm sorry. The latest I can give you is noon," the desk clerk tells me.

"Here's my challenge," I say. "I have a speaking gig this morning, and I don't even get off stage until noon. I will get back to the hotel as soon as I can. I will try to be out by 12:45."

"Once again, I am sorry sir, but we are not offering late checkouts today. We have a conference coming in," she repeated with a dismissive air of condescension in her voice.

"If you cannot check out at that time, we will have to charge you for another night."

I shrugged. "You are welcome to charge me, then," I said, matter-of-fact. "I don't have any way to get back here sooner, and I am late as it is. In fact, I think I'll just stay the extra night that I paid for and that convention attendee will have lost the room for the night. Is that the outcome you were looking for?"

"Um, let me talk to my manager," she said and came back twenty seconds later. "1:00 pm will be fine."

If someone has a legitimate need and you have the ability to accommodate, then be a good person and do what you can to make it work. I wasn't asking for three hours. I was asking for one hour past the normal time. The hotel staff would be cleaning hundreds of rooms, and not everyone was asking for the same accommodation. Let people keep their dignity, and don't make us beg, for crying out loud!

If someone needs to use the restroom, but hasn't bought anything from you, don't tell that person no. Be a good person. Point the way and smile. My God, someone needs to use the restroom! What is wrong with you? Refusing the use of your restroom is one of the most short-sighted and offensive policies that companies employ.

"We aren't here for the public to take advantage of us," you say. "This is a business, for crying out loud!"

Nobody is trying to take advantage. Your parents would be ashamed of you. We've all heard heartbreaking stories of a cruel teacher who wouldn't give a kid permission to go to the restroom and the kid was humiliated in front of the class. If you have a bathroom restriction policy, that cruel person is you. People need to go to the bathroom. Let them.

How many times have you made some stupid, small purchase at a retailer or restaurant just so they would let you use the restroom? Okay, Sparky, you just made forty-five cents. Do you feel better now? I will never come back and spend real dollars, but you got the forty-five cents, didn't you?

A coffee shop had a brilliant note posted on its glass door. It read:

You might not be a customer here today, but this is clearly a moment of need for you. So you are very welcome to use our restrooms. While you are here, if you'd like to buy a cup of coffee, please do. We think it's the best in town!

Brilliant, kind, and human. Do you think they created goodwill with both their customers and future customers? Did you notice that didn't say "non-customers"? Because if they weren't customers before, they are about to be! This act of empathy on the part of this business owner or manager is unfortunately the exception rather than the rule—and that is what makes it so exceptional!

Look at every reason you and your team say "no" to customers, and try to find a way to say yes. Sure, there will be many times you simply can't or don't want to accommodate. It often doesn't make sense. There are some very legitimate legal, ethical, logistical, or even preferential reasons why sometimes the answer has to be no:

"I'm not going to offer meat choices at my vegan restaurant."

"No, I'm not going to send you pictures of my housekeeping staff so you can choose the pretty one you'd like."

"We can't move twenty-two passengers on this flight to different seats so your volleyball team can sit together."

But I guarantee that you get requests every day or every week that you decline, but could easily accommodate. I began this book by reminding you that the biggest source of lost revenue was the customer or client you never knew about. These customers, whom you *do* know about, are often right in front of you or on the phone with you. You have them right where you want them. You have marketed to them, communicated with them, and elicited the one behavior that is crucial to your success: you got them on the phone, in your door, or on your website. You have earned that "golden moment." Don't blow it by telling them no!

The ugly cousin of no is inflexibility or hiding behind policy.

There was a time when the customer was king or queen. For many today, it seems as if the policy manual rules. The rules rule, and any deviation would require actual thought, considerations, and effort.

When your policies are designed so that your staff doesn't have to think, you've eliminated opportunities for them to solve problems and accommodate your customers. Not every situation is covered by your handbook and not every company-driven policy applies to every customer or client. When a good customer—hell, *any* customer—asks for an accommodation, a special request, a forbearance, or flexibility, it should at least be considered and not merely dismissed out of hand.

If your company doesn't permit its employees to wear hats, but a young woman's religion requires that she wears a hijab—let her be who she is! If a client can't meet during business hours because he is a single dad with an inflexible boss and works until 5:00 p.m., then stay late and meet him at 5:30 p.m. And if a sixty-year-old woman walks into your store carrying a steaming six-dollar cup of coffee in a closed coffee cup that she just bought, don't tell her, "Sorry, we don't allow food or drinks in the store." Treat her like an adult. Treat her like a cherished customer and worry more about pleasing her than whether she violated your policy detailed on your paper sign on the wall. Replace any policies that are not directly related to health or safety with guidelines.

This is an actual conversation overheard at a national massage/spa chain:

"I need to put my membership on hold for about a year," the customer said to the young woman behind the counter. "I'm undergoing treatments for a recent cancer diagnosis."

"Okay, you can do that, but you will lose the sessions that you have paid for but haven't used yet," the employee says.

"Really?" the woman responded. "I have been undergoing cancer treatment for the past four months and physically haven't been able to come in. I thought I could save up the ones in my account. Here is a note from my doctor and proof of my treatment."

"I do understand," the employee said sympathetically. "But it's our policy. We do have an option to keep the sessions you have on your account. For thirty dollars a month, you get to keep the ones you have, but we won't add any more."

"So wait. I have to pay thirty dollars a month to keep the ones I have already paid for?" she asked incredulously.

"Yeah. It's our policy. Sorry."

I honestly feel sorry for both of them in that conversation. The employee was restrained by her company, unable to do what she likely wanted to and felt like she should do. The customer was fighting the battle of her life, and this massage/spa chain added insult to injury.

To be fair, I doubt the chain's corporate leadership envisioned a scenario like this, but that's a poor excuse. Their inflexible policy left the employee with no option to deal with an extraordinary situation. Take the time to envision almost every imaginable scenario, and train your people accordingly.

And don't give me the "We can't plan for every situation!" line. I don't buy it. That's a convenient cop-out so you don't have to go through the trouble to plan for most of what is predictable at one time or another and empower your people to deal with the rest. What's the better option? *Not* equipping your people? The simple option is to create a blanket policy that covers everything, right? "If we don't let our people make decisions, then they won't make a wrong decision!" Terrible thinking.

The other argument, once again, is the fallback "slippery slope" cop-out: "If we let this person do it, then we have to let everyone do it!" What? No, you don't. Be a human being. Be compassionate. Be accommodating! Not every scenario involves a customer with cancer, but it doesn't negate the fact that different scenarios require a different answer or level of flexibility. You are not in business to make life easier for your staff. Your business's success is dependent on making life better for your customers.

My brilliant colleague and Hall of Fame Speaker Tim Gard (look him up!) has a wonderful and humorous solution for encountering inflexible policies. He carries his own personal policy manual with him. When an unwitting hotel front-desk clerk tells him no to a question and quotes corporate policy to him, Tim pulls a small booklet from his pocket and says: "Well, my policy manual says, 'Yes.' It clearly states it right here . . ." as he holds open a page with the word "Yes" in bold letters. The desk clerk looks bewildered and then laughs. Most often, that's all it takes for the clerk to give in. Hilarious. Better still—effective!

The point is that inflexible policies are bad business. The success of Nordstrom's legendary customer service can be traced directly to their frontline staff who are equipped and emboldened to solve problems. The answer for them is always yes. It almost doesn't matter what the question is. They are given the freedom to make it right—and they don't need to get a manager.

For frontline workers, the easiest thing when confronted with an unfamiliar situation is to just say, "No," or "Sorry, I'm afraid we can't," and then move on. Big mistake. How about empowering your people to find a way to say yes? Or if they have to say no, offer an alternative that both can agree to. Not only do you save an important client or customer relationship, but you get to be the hero for solving a problem. Customers remember and they reward you with positive reviews and future business.

WHY YOU DO IT:

Many in business adopt some measure of the franchise model. The franchise is centered around predictability. The more things we can standardize and control, the more things we can predict, and the fewer things can go awry. And if we can reduce straying from the anticipated scenarios, it's easier to manage our business, create budgets, and pay our bills.

However, the cost of managing for predictability is the lost opportunities from better navigating unanticipated scenarios. We lose opportunities to accommodate our customers (who are often just being human), and we lose many of those customers from the frustration generated by our inflexibility.

WHY WE HATE IT:

We don't like being told no. Worse yet, when we can conceive of simple scenarios that would involve some measure of concession but others don't see it, refuse to see it, or see it but still say no, we are frustrated. In our mind, a simple accommodation seems reasonable. When you don't offer that accommodation, we view you as unreasonable—and we don't like doing business with unreasonable people.

A BETTER APPROACH:

Eliminate the word "no" from your company's vocabulary. Either replace it with "It would be my pleasure!" or some version of "Here's what we can do." Create a culture of problem-solving and accommodation. It doesn't mean that every customer gets what they want, the way they want it every time, but they should get something. Redirect your efforts to discover and communicate what you can do. People will often understand that you can't do something if you offer an alternative or some level of accommodation.

Gather your team for a brainstorming session. Order in food, put your cell phones on vibrate, and roll up your sleeves. Walk through every familiar and unfamiliar scenario with your customers, clients, or patients, and discuss all the times you say no. Categorize them into three sections: (1) Have to say no; (2) offer an alternative; and (3) find a way to say yes. Chart all the ideas and plot them into one of the three sections. Role-play both likely and unlikely scenarios. Equip and empower your team to think-on-the-fly and effectively deal with the scenarios they confront.

Work together to not only anticipate unusual scenarios, but to truly understand your customers, why they are making the request, what our flexibility would mean to them, and what their satisfaction would mean to us. The value of the exercise is in the process itself. When we help our people to understand what the "extra mile" and flexibility means to our customers and their satisfaction, our people will often understand and rise to the occasion.

2

DON'T FAKE IT UNTIL YOU MAKE IT

I am not qualified to talk about the diet,
simply because I am not a dietician.
–Nine-time Olympic Gold Medal swimmer Mark Spitz

We've often heard the line: *Fake it until you make it.* In its most innocent form, it's a simple admonition for people aspiring to higher levels to just get in there and do the work that others are already doing at those levels in order to prove yourself. I understand the motivation, intent, and aspirational application. But when it comes to business, the temptation to "fake" anything is a slippery slope.

"We'll figure it out!" they say. "Give us your business and we'll find a way to make it happen."

And while on some level, it's admirable that a business is willing to do what it takes to make the customer happy and fulfill their end of the bargain, is it really ethical to figure it out on someone else's dime? Shouldn't you only accept business when you know you can hit it out of the park? Wouldn't it be better (safer) to refer that prospect to someone who knows the business, has some relevant experience, and can guarantee delivery?

As a professional speaker, I am frequently asked if I can speak on a subject that is related to my traditional topics of marketing and customer experience, but with some variation. If it involves simply tailoring the message to a particular industry, that's what I do for every client. The answer is a robust "Yes!"

But if the request is for a different subject altogether, for example, leadership, teamwork, change management, or motivation, then I always decline and refer them to a trusted colleague who I know could crush it for them. It's not that I don't have knowledge and experience in all those subjects, it's just not my primary business. There are others who would do a better job. I could do a presentation or workshop for them, and it would be fine, but I don't do fine. I only do great. I only do outstanding. That's not ego talking. It's commitment. My clients and audiences pay me for great. Anything less then great, and my clients would be underwhelmed and likely complain about me to others. Anything less than great, and I would risk my reputation—and my livelihood.

When you agree to do work that you are not qualified to do, you are shooting yourself (and your client) in the foot. Better put, when you attempt to earn money from work you may not be able to deliver, it's like peeing in your pants. (Stay with me here.) It'll give you a warm feeling for a moment, but it's not going to do you much good in the long run. At best, you'll "pull it off" and escape unscathed. At worst, you'll appear as if you've scammed your client. They won't forget it and will likely tell others.

The beloved Broadway musical and film *The Music Man* tells the story of professor Harold Hill, who travels from town to town convincing the townsfolk that they need to form a boy's band to keep the youth out of trouble. He convinces them to buy expensive uniforms and band instruments, but he has no skills in actually teaching music or leading the band. By the time they figure out the ruse, he's off to the next town.

In the musical, a traveling salesman recognizes "Professor" Hill and outs him to the town leaders. He is ultimately captured and has to face the people he has swindled. Of course, because its a musical, there is redemption, love, spontaneous singing, group dancing, and a happy ending. But in real life, underperformers are outed much more quickly and pay a heavy price. Today, we use the Internet to "out" underperformers. With resources like Yelp, TripAdvisor, Angie's List, HomeAdvisor, Rotten Tomatoes, Glassdoor, and others, we share both positive and negative reviews. If you perform anywhere below the top of your game, someone will tell your story—to everyone.

Of course, there is no real truth-test for Internet reviews, and nefarious forces can conspire to negatively impact your business. As of this writing, there is not yet a filter to address this. The Internet is the Wild West of both wonderful stories and tall tales, accurate reflections and gross exaggerations. And while you can't guarantee the accuracy of a review, you can almost guarantee that those who feel underserved will share their displeasure. Like all things Internet, the recounting of their bad experience will live on and on.

At the most basic level, we expect you to say what you'll do, and do what you say. Swindlers of one sort or another have always been around—from the traveling snake-oil salesmen of the old West to the well-documented, modern-day roofing scammers that follow natural disasters around the country and promise to repair your roof, only to disappear days later. I'm not sure if there are more scammers in today's world or if modern media is bringing more of them to our attention, but we've learned to be on our guard. We're conditioned to be skeptical.

When Denver's shiny new airport opened in February of 1995, relief was the predominant feeling expressed. As glorious as the new tent-roofed structure was, the fact remained that it opened years later than originally planned and a full sixteen months after everything was completed. Everything, that is, except for the new, state-of-the-art baggage system. With seventeen miles of tracks and five miles of conveyor belts, this first-of-its-kind baggage system was promised to increase speed and efficiency by eliminating the traditional tug and trolley system.

Not only did the new system not work correctly, but images of luggage being destroyed, carts crashing into each other, and other malfunctions flashed across television sets around the world. As BAE Systems (now bankrupt) worked to solve the problems, the new airport sat for sixteen months at a cost of over a million dollars a day to the City of Denver. They never got the system to work.

There was plenty of blame to go around. BAE Systems sold a system they had never actually built but believed they could deliver. The city took a big chance on a shiny technology that was unproven, and Denver's hub airlines banked on a competitive advantage that this new, expensive system would provide. Food vendors who signed leases at the new airport also bought equipment and had to pay their vendors with no incoming revenue. Everyone lost.

Another travel-related example is how airlines get away every day with their spotty (and that's being generous) in-flight Wi-Fi service. Here's my question: How can you legally sell a service when you can never guarantee it's consistent delivery?

"Sorry," the busy flight attendant will say, shrugging. "It's apparently not working." Knowing that she's trapped with a flight full of frustrated business travelers with work to do, she can only mime the same response to everyone. She's had a lot of practice.

The frustration stems from more than just the unavailability of a promised service, but from the fact that often passengers don't find out until after they've paid for the service. The airlines simply pocket the money without delivering the service. We get mad enough when we are told no, but we are furious when we pay for something and are then told "Sorry, you won't be getting what you've paid for."

Adding insult to injury, we are told that *we* have to go online, navigate the refund policy, fill out their form, and apply for a refund. The burden is shifted to the slighted (robbed) customer to fix something that the company should make right. (This will be covered more in Chapter 16.) The airlines know full well that the vast majority of travelers will not take the time to go online and navigate the process to recover $8.99 or $17.99. The customer is dissatisfied (angry), and the company is enriched without ever having to provide the service they promised and charged for. Something is seriously wrong with this picture.

First-world problem? Of course it is! But don't miss the point. It's not that we should be grateful that we have the miracle of Internet connection aboard the miracle of flight. This is about commerce and contract. If something is offered and charged for, it must be delivered. If you can't deliver it, then you shouldn't be allowed to charge for it. It's true for your business and it's true for mine. It's called fraud. There should be a law against that. Oh yeah, there is.

The only companies that can generally get away with underdelivering are those that provide services or products for transient customers or a captive audience. In other words, they know we are likely never coming back or we have nowhere else to go. At an amusement park, we have to pay their food prices because we have no other option. Tourist spots or airport restaurants can get away with poor service because we are likely never coming back—or so they tell themselves. But even those providers are subject to our sharing stories of dissatisfaction.

The message here is simple: The fastest way to guarantee poor word-of-mouth is to fail to deliver on your promise. And the way to increase the likelihood of failing to deliver is to promise something that you are unqualified or ill-equipped to provide.

A gentleman approached me after a speaking gig and told me a story about his father, who was a traveling lingerie salesman in the 1940s (true story). His dad would take his sales case filled with ladies' undergarments and visit women's clothing stores across the country, driving from store to store, taking orders. The man's father would occasionally take him along on driving trips, promising dinner at a restaurant (a big deal during tough economic times) and a stay in a hotel. He watched his father sell and listened to his pitch.

On one occasion, a small clothing store owner liked a particular garment and she ordered two dozen. Surprisingly, his father told her, "Just order one dozen. If you need more, just call, and I will have them shipped."

In the car later, the boy asked his father why he would turn down that big sale. His father responded, "Son, I know these products, and there is no way she would have sold all of them. I'll be passing through this town again in six months. If she hasn't sold them, then she will think that my products aren't good and she'll never buy again. I'd rather sell her what she needs rather than what I need her to buy. If I can deliver what I promised, then she'll buy from me forever."

Brilliant business lesson! If you plan to be in business next year and the year after, then play the long game. Only sell what you know you can deliver.

WHY YOU DO IT:

People are eager for business. We have bills to pay and we need to work. I don't think most people set out intending to fail or underdeliver on their promises. To the contrary, most in business truly believe they can come through for their clients. But the truth is, not everyone who has done something has the ability to do it for others at a high level. Just because you Snapchat your friends and get hundreds of likes on your Instagram post doesn't mean that you are a so-cial media marketing expert who can help companies grow their business.

You are only an expert after you've earned it, after you've demonstrated competency and expertise in the marketplace by successfully doing the work you promised. You can pitch the business when you have a track record, sufficient staff, and bandwidth to complete the tasks you've contracted for.

WHY WE HATE IT:

We trusted you, and you failed to deliver as we expected. You claimed to be able to do something that you weren't able to provide at the level you promised, or when you promised. 'Nuff said.

A BETTER APPROACH:

Don't pursue or accept any work that you can't deliver at a very high level or in a timely fashion. At the very least, partner with another professional or firm with the necessary experience, resources, and capabilities to ensure satisfaction.

If you want to expand your service offerings, then get training, build your skills, or volunteer/apprentice with others to learn a new skill. Don't simply guess before you accept work. Know! Sometimes the best way to make a lot of money, in the long run, is to reject money for work you can't crush in the short term. It's far better to lose a sale than to lose your reputation.

3

Automation Kills Loyalty

*It's so much more powerful to aim for the
smallest possible audience, not the largest.*
–Seth Godin

Just a generation ago, a trip to the mailbox brought a sense of anticipation. Will there be a letter from a loved one who moved far away? A thank-you note from a friend? A postcard from a relative traveling overseas? Or maybe an invitation to a party or wedding!

In short order, those eagerly anticipated social correspondence were overtaken by obligations in our mailbox. Bills began to make their way into that sacred space, crowding out the letters. Soon, a trip to the mailbox carried with it a sense of dread, knowing full well what was waiting for us. As advertising began to transition from the newspapers and

Yellow Pages to the mailbox, the volume grew and grew, and the term "junk mail" became a part of the public lexicon.

Flash forward: The Internet and electronic mail (email) brought with it the promise of vast efficiency and cost savings. "Why spend thousand of dollars printing and mailing promotional material," business owners said to themselves, "when I can design it online and email for a fraction of the cost?" In fact, emailing your advertisements to hundreds of thousands of prospects costs less than snail mailing to those in your neighborhood. "Where is the downside?" business owners asked.

Well, it doesn't take a rocket scientist to foresee where this would go. The volumes of junk mail that we used to throw away from our mailbox just morphed into the "spam" that we now ignore and delete from our always-full email inbox. The dozen of items that used to fill our mailbox, limited in part by the hard costs of printing and mailing, have become hundreds of daily emails trying to pitch us (or fool us). And this doesn't even count all those captured by our spam filters!

So, all this begs the question: If you are annoyed and frustrated by the onslaught of unwanted emails, why do you think that your prospects will respond positively to your using the same methodology?

The correlation is irrefutable: The rise of automation and efficiency has brought with it a corresponding decrease in personalization and legitimate connection. Worse still, mass email often creates frustration and even outright hostility.

To be clear, not every correspondence is intended to create a deeper connection. Often efficiency and the ability to expedite communication is the primary driver. The electronic delivery of monthly bills and newsletters (e-zines) are a cost-effective and efficient way to deliver materials and information. Instantaneous bank fraud alerts and notification from motion detectors at your home or place of business make great use of electronic communication.

The challenge comes when the efficiency of your communication interferes with your ability to truly connect and generate the interest or inquiry you desire. How you intend the outreach to be received is almost irrelevant. How it is received and perceived is purely in the mind of the recipient.

While you may be thrilled with your new customer relationship management (CRM) system that allows for email blasts to thousands or even millions of targeted prospects, just know that those on the receiving end are fully (painfully) aware that your message isn't just for them. True, you might have a mail-merge feature to get their name right, but the message is meant for the masses, and we know that.

Most often, your goal is to get a response that will lead to a phone call, a visit to your website, or even a trip to your location. Most often, the results are sporadic at best. An expected and acceptable response rate for the old-style direct-mail postcards or brochures was 4 percent. Advertisers were willing to accept a response rate that low to justify the printing and mailing costs. That number was a function, in part, of casting a wide net. Not everyone in that neighborhood needs a new dry cleaner, replacement windows, or chiropractic care. A 4 percent response was a good number and reflected accurate demographic targeting and effective messaging. Any number above or below that was a direct reflection of doing a better or worse job in regard to those two factors.

Response rates for email blasts are a tiny fraction of that. And while you may be just fine with a very, very low level of response as the email costs are far lower than traditional mailing, you are missing a bigger picture and a much bigger pie. In other words, do you know what you are losing for the cost-effective gains you are seeing? Are you in a position to write off 99.9 percent of your potential prospects in order to efficiently reach the .01 percent who will actually respond?

Here is the fact: When you send email blasts, you have no idea how many of the prospects who ignored you, were annoyed by you, and deleted you might actually have connected with you if they had been approached in a more personal way. You have no way of knowing. Ignorance isn't bliss. It's lost revenue.

The question is: Are you so successful that you can afford to annoy 99 percent of your prospects?

Every year, I receive dozens of holiday greeting cards from friends, clients, business associates, and even from some loyal fans. My staff dutifully displays them in the office, and we are truly appreciative of those who appreciate us and take the time to reach out at the end of the year. What astonishes me, however, is that about one third of them are digitally generated. To be clear, the cards are beautiful, with lovely designs and warm sentiments included, but there are no actual signatures. Often, it's just a company name and perhaps some preprinted staff signatures. A staff person ordered them online and just uploaded a mailing list for the printer to send to.

Why on Earth would companies go through the trouble and expense of sending warm holiday greetings, intended to create connection and convey gratitude, but do it in the most time and cost-efficient way possible? It's akin to sending your assistant out to buy your kid a birthday present or programming an autoresponder to say "Thank You" to everyone who just did business with you. It's certainly efficient, but you lose the message for the messenger.

My colleague Eric Chester offers that this is just another way of saying, "When you care enough to do the very least." It would be funny if it weren't so true.

Honestly, it's better to not send a card at all, rather than use an approach that elicits cynicism or head-shaking. It's better that your customers think nothing than believe that you are cheap and impersonal.

When was the last time you received a handwritten letter or thank-you note? Better still, when was the last time you wrote one? I'm not suggesting that you can replace mass emails with large numbers of handwritten notes. I'm saying you should do more of one and less of the other. Depending on the value of a client in your business, the two minutes it takes to write a note or even five minutes to personalize a typed letter can make a world of difference in how it is received.

Products like InfusionSoft and other complex email-marketing platforms offer great efficiency to reach large numbers of customers and prospects, but I would caution you to reflect on what you use these tools for. I think they are much more effective to keep in contact with those who already know and love you, but woefully ineffective with those you hope will work with you in the future.

Quite simply (and none of this is simple), don't spend time and money on things that create negative feelings toward you and your business.

Political candidates who interrupt my dinner with robocalls lose my support. Is anybody truly influenced to change their position by a voice on a robocall? More are likely repelled. Professionals who add me to their email lists without my permission get deleted. Local professionals who mail form-letter pitches fall off my radar. Social media connections who tag me along with ninety others in a post that has nothing to do with me get unfriended. I simply don't want to work with or buy from people who see me as a faceless target.

Do you think I am taking this way too personally? Trust when I say that I am not. In fact, I care so little about people who don't care about me and my family that I barely give them a second thought. Isn't your goal just the opposite? Aren't you trying to engage me, interest me, and get me to connect with and respond to you? The opposite of love isn't hate. It's indifference. Indifference is to business what a member of the computer club is to the prom queen. You're not even on our radar.

Business is like high school. When given the choice, we do business with people we like and people we trust. We trust people who take the time to know something about us, speak directly to us, and thank us for our time. We like people who like us. People who like us don't spam us.

P. T. Barnum famously opined that there's a sucker born every minute. The truth is that we rarely respond to your mass marketing because we don't want to feel like a sucker. We don't want you to think we were taken in by your pitch or scam. Regardless of whether your pitch was intended as or appears in any way to be a scam, it is often taken that way. Simply, in the interest of time, you are thrown into the trash (deleted) with the rest of the spam. We rarely even take the time to read it.

WHY YOU DO IT:

You send mass emails for the cost and time savings achieved, pure and simple. You have been lured by technology and efficiency and have justified the impersonal nature by deluding yourself that the mail-merge feature will achieve personalization. Trust me. They will notice the lack of meaningful information about them, their business, or the specific challenges they face.

The responses you do get will often reinforce in your mind that the return on investment was financially worthwhile. What you undervalue is the cost to your reputation and brand, which are essentially the same thing.

You automate to reach more people in less time for less money. Your emails reach hundreds of thousands. Your calls reach countless homes and require little to no staff time. It seems like a smart and efficient way to do business. The bean counters are happy. Your cost per contact plunges, and your marketing reaches the masses like never before. However . . .

WHY WE HATE IT:

Quite simply, we are overwhelmed by the crap that fills our email inbox. The spam is overwhelming, and so we tune it out. We delete quickly and often. Those that spam us (maybe not your intention, but certainly our perception) are not just thrown in a mental bucket of being disposable and dismissible, but also classified as annoying and intrusive—two words you do not want attached to your name. We think, "Why does so and so keep sending me this junk?" Then, if you ever do have an opportunity for a legitimate connection, we are already predisposed against you.

A BETTER APPROACH:

Balance. Balance efficiency with effectiveness—and effectiveness is not a measure of how many people you reach. It is a measure of how many of them do, act, and feel the way you want them to. An effective outreach is one that elicits positive feelings toward your brand. It generates interest from your prospects and leads to connection, engagement, and sales.

Automate for pedestrian tasks. Automate when you have no need or desire to influence, but merely to deliver or notify. Personalize when you are educating, persuading, enlightening, and soliciting. Delivered authentically, your results will reward your effort.

4

Don't Close—Ever

Opportunity doesn't knock. It plays Ding-Dong Ditch!
—Author

In yesteryear, when we wanted to buy something, we drove to a place of business, parked, went inside, and looked for our item. Then we brought our selection to the counter and the clerk rang it up. We had to plan ahead to make sure we got there during business hours, and if they were closed, we waited until they opened again. The physical presence of the merchant or an employee was required for commerce to take place.

In the early twentieth century, catalogues allowed people in rural areas to mail in their orders and buy items that city dwellers had easy access to through larger merchants like Sears Roebuck, Woolworths, Montgomery Ward, and others.

And while they saved themselves the trouble of a long journey to the big city, the tradeoff was a long wait—often weeks —for the items to arrive.

Throughout most of the nineteenth and twentieth centuries, keeping our money in banks offered safety for our hard-earned cash, but there was tradeoff: You could only get access to your money during banking hours. Personal checks and credit cards gave us a substitute for cash, but banking hours still restricted easy access to our money. If you wanted money, you had to go to the bank—when they were open.

The advent of the automatic teller machine (ATM) in 1967, and their first widespread use in the 1970s, was a revolution. Being able to finally access our bank accounts in the evenings and on weekends transformed our lives. Well, at the least, it freed up our weekends by putting cash in our pockets. It's not that we couldn't spend on the weekends in earlier years, we just had to plan ahead.

Even weekend hours is a fairly new concept as many stores were historically closed on the weekend. Sunday hours were virtually unheard of, with the exception of restaurants and movie theaters. Retailers who extended their hours created a strong competitive advantage over others in their spaces. Inevitably, competitors followed suit, and weekend hours became the norm.

It wasn't until the always-on Internet that business became truly twenty-four seven. Not only can you now access a company's website, but the advent of e-commerce tools allow for secure purchases over the Internet. Even though most have been slow to offer total access to their products and services after hours, there are enough players in each space that do, and alternatives are not hard to find—even at 2:00 a.m.

The point is that we are living in a dramatically different world. We have come to expect access to everything we want, whenever we want it. In most cases, we can get it. If we can't get it from you, then we will get it from your competitors, plain and simple. And when you open for business the next day, draw back the curtains, and unlock the door, we are already lost to you—because we purchased from someone else the evening before or had our questions answered. The need has been met, and we are long gone.

We can search online at all hours of the night, and when we find something that we want to buy, we will find someone who will take our money. If there is no option to reach you or buy from you, we will buy from someone else. When we decide to seek out a service provider for household repairs or other tasks, we often will hire the first one that actually answers the phone. That's it. Literally hired for no other reason than that person was available to respond when we called. That's how impatient we are. Even if we leave you a message (we rarely will), by the time you have responded, we have likely found what we were looking for and already made our purchase or appointment.

Consider this: It is estimated that only about 15 percent of companies today have adopted an always-on business model to support their always-connected customers.

Of course, there are legitimate reasons for the plethora of late-night inquiries: It's moms and dads who are finding time for themselves or to catch up on set-aside tasks after the kids are finally in bed. Students doing late-night research or connecting on social media. Entrepreneurs burning the midnight oil, solving the business problems of the day, or anyone just sifting through emails during a fit of insomnia.

Don't dismiss this as just the "as seen on TV shoppers." It's any of us, and at times, it's all of us.

As an international professional speaker and business consultant, my business never closes. Ever! Calls and email inquiries come in twenty-four seven from prospects and clients around the world. This is not to say that we never get a break. Calls aren't constantly interrupting our evenings out or late-night sleep. But if a prospect from Singapore or Dubai wants to speak at 2:00 a.m., they get a live person, or at least a quick response. We know that in many cases, we are not the only speaker or consultant they are considering. If we respond quicker, we will often get the gig. In many cases, the other professionals that they were considering never even had a chance to compete. We've already responded and sealed the deal before they even picked up the message.

It's stunning to me how many businesses have a contact form on their websites, but no other way to reach them directly. Not only will most prospects refuse to fill out the form, but even if they do, the response will often be too late. Prospects don't patiently wait for all the responses to come in, weigh them each carefully, and then reach out over the coming days. When they find a professional or vendor that meets their needs, they stop looking.

When finding a lost item, people always say, "It was in the last place I looked!" Of course it was! When you found it, you stopped looking. So it is with service providers. As my kids say, "You snooze, you lose." (Actually, everyone says that.)

It's mind-boggling how many service businesses provide office phone numbers on their websites and business cards, but no way to reach them after hours. To be clear, you have every right to draw a line of distinction between work and home, obligation and personal time. Just know that when you close your business, others are getting your clients because they were available to talk when the prospect wanted to. That is a trade-off you may be at peace with. I respect that.

However, is having to close your business in favor of family time really the only option that you have? Have you explored the cost of a live chat feature on your website? Are you fully cognizant of the after-hours answering services and the new technologies that make the transition to virtual staff virtually seamless? Have you considered adopting e-commerce platforms that allow for some types of purchases online?

I get the balance thing. My family time is very sacred for me, but I have made arrangements to ensure that no client goes unserved, or opportunity lost, merely because my time zone doesn't match theirs. My family also understands that while I have the flexibility to attend most school functions and can adjust my schedule more than most, late calls or an occasional interrupted dinner could also mean a cool trip with Daddy later in the year.

Business today is not just twenty-four seven because your prospects are up at all hours of the night. It's because your prospects are likely around the world. They are sleeping while you are up working, and they are buying while you sleep. And as satellite views of the Earth show clusters of bright city lights begin to dim as people go to sleep for the night, the Internet is always alive with that soft glow, always humming with activity, inquiries, views, posts, and purchases. Right now, your participation is an option. Soon, it will be a necessity. I maintain that you can gain a competitive advantage today by finding ways to be open—*always!*

In the 1970s, Tupperware pointed to their prolific global reach and claimed that "somewhere, at every moment of every day or night, somewhere in the world, someone is hosting a Tupperware Party."

Today, that same adage holds true for virtually every industry. Billions of people are buying at every moment of every day—and not just online. Can they buy from you, reach you, ask questions of you, search your products or services, and learn all they want to know from you whenever *they* want to? If they can't, you are losing out to competitors who provide these options.

Even if your industry does not traditionally allow for after-hours access, for example, bowling, teeth bleaching, tax preparation, breast augmentation, or a haircut, at the very least prospects should be able to get the information they want, make reservations, or pay their bills at the hour of their choosing.

Don't make us wait until you are open for business. We won't. Don't ask us to leave a message. We won't. Do your best to not place us on hold while you help another customer. Chances are, we won't. We're not rude. We're busy. It's not personal. We just don't need you. You're not one in a million. You're one *of* a million.

WHY YOU DO IT:

Most in business offer specific, limited business hours for three reasons: the business model doesn't lend itself to extended hours; the additional cost of staffing after hours can be prohibitive; and the need to draw a line between work hours and family time. Quite simply, you need time off and time away from work. I get it.

Most in business simply haven't taken the time to explore alternative staffing and quick response methodologies. Whether you are fearful of the costs involved or simply unaware of the plethora of alternatives, you close because you feel you need to. The work day is over. Time to close up shop.

WHY WE HATE IT:

We have become conditioned in recent years to having instantaneous access to products, vendors, and information. If we want something at 3:00 a.m., Amazon can get it for us in a day—or less. If we need facts and figures, we search Google, or ask Siri or Alexa. When you are not available when we want you, you are saying "no" to us—and we don't like no. We are looking for current, and you are looking so 1985.

A BETTER APPROACH:

Explore ways to be available for your customers and prospects whenever they need you and want you, even if it is not you. There are ways of replicating yourself by staffing with alternative methodologies. Offer weekend hours and extended evening hours, and have employees staff the business. Often the additional revenue from being an available choice for customers during nontraditional hours will more than offset the additional cost.

Until you have the resources to be available twenty-four seven, find a way to at least be responsive. Hire overseas talent to staff a live chat feature. If they have to leave a message, give a guaranteed window of time when your company will respond—and honor it. Provide payment options that allow for after-hours purchases, or a place to click-to-schedule a slot on your calendar for a specific time to talk or meet.

The point is that the longer you wait for the inevitable shift to an always-open model (that is already taking place in many industries), the more you will be playing catch-up to those who have already made the investment or are making plans to extend their hours and the availability of their products, services, time, and expertise. Oh, look! Here comes another prospect. Don't blink!

5

Don't Be Hard to Reach

*I dial up the suicide prevention hotline, get a busy
signal, and wonder if that's a sign of the times.*
–Troy James Weaver

So, why would I need an entire chapter to relate a simple
admonition like "Don't be hard to get in touch with"?
This sounds pretty basic and self-explanatory. But the truth
is that companies have both overt and subtle ways of creating barriers between themselves and their customers. Some
cause annoyance, while others elicit rage. Neither supports
desired loyalty and customer retention. A greater exploration is in order. First, a reminder of basic human nature:

Since the dawn of humanity, we have craved answers
to basic questions. For early man, it was understanding the
best ways to find food, keep warm, anticipate danger, protect

our families, and understanding why on Earth Gronk would think he has a chance to mate with Oog, when Oog is clearly out of his league.

As time went on, we used our intelligence, tools, and resources to discover answers. Some of the questions were basic, while others took a lifetime to discover. Answering questions moved us forward as a species. We encountered problems and found ways to solve them. We got better, invented stuff, discovered things, and made life better for our families and humanity. When we couldn't find an answer, we pushed harder, searched harder, got more resourceful, and found a way. Our continued existence, growth, and culture has been defined by our search and discovery for answers to questions.

But what if there was only one source to find the answer to a pressing question? What if you absolutely need an answer to solve an important problem, but there was only one way to get it? Maybe you need to clarify something about your health insurance, but getting that question answered would require holding your phone to your ear for an hour. And during that hour, you would have no guarantee or confidence that anyone would ever actually answer the phone.

What if you were considering an expensive purchase, but the company made a conscious decision to refuse to provide a phone number or an email address, so you couldn't contact them directly? Perhaps that company offered only a contact form that didn't allow for image uploads, attachments, signature lines, direction to a particular department, or any level of deviation or elaboration. Just a simple message in a box on their form. Would that endear you to that high-end retailer?

The dichotomy is both stark and profoundly impactful: Companies have a laundry list of reasons why they would like to restrict access to a real person, yet customers almost always prefer to talk to a real person. They simply don't want to let you contact them the way that you want to, yet they want you to buy from them, except you can't reach them to answer your questions, but they talk about appreciating their customers, except they understaff their customer service phone lines and make you wait . . . a long time.

There is a disconnect between the words and the actions such that it appears beyond disingenuous. We have become cynical to company claims because the offenses are so pervasive. The worst part is that few in business would acknowledge they are primary offenders. They think it's always others, not them. Really? Here are a few questions that might (should) make you rethink your innocence. In your business:

Does a real person pick up the phone by the third ring? What? Does that seem unrealistic? Well, do *you* hold on through the fourth ring when you are calling someone? Most people will hang up. Pick up your phone and talk to your customers! Whose job is it to answer the phone in your company? Everyone's! Whose job is it to pick us a piece of trash on the floor in your business? Everyone's!

Do you force your customers/clients to navigate your voice menu system to find the person or department they are looking for? Do they have to listen to endless instructions and then wait to "press 6" and then "press 4" and then "press 8" to return to the main menu and then leave a message? Could that two-minute call, with frustration building, have been directed by a real person in less than ten seconds? (The answer is yes.)

Does your website include phone numbers to directly reach the person or department they need? Can they go directly to your contact information from the home page? From every page? Keep in mind, however, that if you include a phone number on your website, and that number takes them to a phone system that takes several minutes to navigate, then it doesn't count!

Does your website direct people to a contact form without also providing the option of a phone number and working email address? If you only include the contact form, you are losing 90 percent of your prospects! They simply will not fill out your form. Nobody wants to fill out a contact form. You don't, so why do you ask your prospects to? The contact form is the answering machine of the internet.

Have you cut costs by understaffing your customer service line, tech support, or billing department so that people have to wait on hold for more than a minute or two? Good news and bad news: The good news is your CFO or finance person is happy. You saved money! Woohoo! The bad news is your customers are unhappy. You lost money. Boo hoo. Happy bookkeeper. Unhappy client. Happy bean counter. Unhappy banker . . . or owner . . . or investors. Are you seeing what is wrong with this picture?

Do you have work-related, unreturned emails that have been in your mailbox for more than three days? I guarantee that the sender of that unreturned email is feeling ignored and insulted. If others are reaching out to you and not getting a quick response, then you are hard to reach. If you have time to keep up with your social media, then you have time to return emails.

Do your customers and prospects have a way to reach someone on your team or get answers to questions after hours? Do you at least have an answering service, live web-chat support, or a twenty-four-hour toll-free customer service line? Even if your business doesn't lend itself to an always-on model (for example, you have a carpet cleaning service or a pizza restaurant), is there an after-hours emergency line? What about food poisoning or a fire?

Do you have a section on your website for frequently asked questions (FAQ)? Are you using that as a crutch to save you from being asked the same questions over and over? Do you recognize that people hate having to take time to search for answers about you and your business? (Especially when they know that you could answer that question quickly.)

Of course, your people are tired of answering the same questions over and over. Yes. *And?* Your customers feeling valued and heard and satisfied that they got their questions answered is far more important than your employees not wanting to answer your customers questions more than once. Why are you in business if it's not to serve your customers? This is beyond basic, friends!

For every three minutes we are on hold, our frustration escalates to a new loyalty-harming level. Our initial annoyance turns into frustration, then to anger, and ultimately, to rage. Then, when we finally get to talk to a customer service agent, we are angry. How sad for that poor agent who is forced to deal with frustrated and furious customers all day long. You know exactly what I am talking about. Are you guilty of this as well?

Professional service providers, or those that provide a facilitated purchase, are particularly at risk because we are already being told that we don't need you. If you are hard to reach, then it just reinforces the point. Carvana says we can buy the car without the car salesperson. Zillow tells us that we don't need a real estate agent. E-Trade allows us to skip the broker. Quicken Loans helps us find a mortgage and never leave our home. So, if we can bypass the agents in our town, why should we wait for you to return our call?

Then there is the issue of the delayed response.

Never before has the phrase "You snooze, you lose" been more true. Blame the growing impatience of your customers or the instantaneous availability of most things we want or need. Regardless, the way we buy has been directly effected.

In yesteryear, we would take some time to explore options, get quotes or prices from a few different vendors, and make our decision. We didn't make our choice too quickly lest we lose out on a better deal. Price or value was the primary driver.

Today, in many instances, expediency has overtaken price as the primary driver of purchase decisions. It's not that price is unimportant. Price is always important, but most of our options are already competitively priced. We can shop our competitors just as our customers can. We know what others charge and we are most often in line with those. So, in an age of price parity, those who can deliver what we want faster often will win the battle.

Our responsiveness and expediency is tied directly to our preferability in the eyes of our customers. Most often, our prospects won't wait for all options before making a decision. The first to respond has a high likelihood of getting the gig—provided they are priced fairly.

This plays out every day on Craigslist. When you reach out to multiple home service vendors on Craigslist, one of those will invariably respond faster than the others. If that tradesperson can do your job, when you want it done and at an agreeable price point, then that vendor will get the gig. Others may not even respond until the end of the day, or days later. Too late. You've already hired someone.

There's a lot of snoozin' and losin' going on in the world today. Wake up.

WHY YOU DO IT:

Most in business create distance between themselves and their customers, not out of any sense of disdain, but as a reaction to the inevitable growing demands on their time as their company grows.

In the early days, when there weren't many customers, it was easy to balance the demands of running the business and dealing with customers. But as the business grows, both the operational and customer service demands grow as well. The internal issues require focus and strategy, while the customer issues often take us "off task." We restrict access to key personnel, lest they be overwhelmed with the minutia. We find ways to answer those pesky questions from our pesky customers with FAQs and dedicated customer support staff. And since those staffers are seen as expenses rather than revenue generators, their numbers have to be managed.

WHY WE HATE IT:

In our minds, we know what the problem is, and we have a pretty good idea of how we would like it solved. Or, we have a simple question, but it is not a "frequently asked question." We are confident that our issue could be resolved, or our questions answered if we can just find a company representative—a real person—to talk to. When we can't reach the person we want . . . well, you know how we feel.

A BETTER APPROACH:

The better approach is hiding in plain sight. At the end of virtually every frustratingly long voicemail menu, after the voice has given us nine different department choices, we hear: "If you'd like to speak with an operator, press zero."

There it is. After you've exhausted all the other options, there is a real person available. It just took a while to get there. It needn't have.

Find a way to help your vital customers (all customers) bypass the garbage and get to a real person. Whenever possible, we have to let our customers do business with us the way *they* would like to. It's not always easy, but their happiness, loyalty, satisfaction, and revenue are worth it.

And even if it is logistically and financially not feasible to staff at the levels that would be required for unlimited access, there are better ways than accepting ridiculous forty-five-minute hold times. Implement surge-staffing strategies during high-demand hours, offer live chat, and rotate senior staff on call so everyone gets a shift to hear from and deal with customer questions and concerns. Finally, always have a phone number and email option on your website.

6

DON'T PEE ON MY LEG AND TELL ME IT'S RAINING

Fool me once, shame on you! Fool me twice, shame on me!
–Randall Terry

In yesteryear, it was often said that a man's handshake was as good as a contract, that his word was his bond. (Pardon the gender-specific reference, but that's how it was said.) A promise was as good as gold.

For generations, we relied on a firm handshake and good eye contact. You didn't trust someone who didn't know how to shake hands. A "dead fish" handshake was not to be trusted and set the relationship off on a bad footing.

Integrity was the foundation of relationships, both personal and professional. They didn't file lawsuits in the old West. They pulled out their guns. You didn't dare steal a horse, lest you be branded a "no good, dirty horse thief," and that was to be a social outcast. And if you cheated in a card game, it was perfectly reasonable to be shot dead for the infraction. It wasn't about the cards. It was about being cheated and lied to. It was an unwritten but widely understood code, and an honorable man didn't do it—or put up with it.

There are those who say that the truth is a tricky thing. If you ask a shady accountant what two plus two is, the accountant might ask, "What do you want it to be?" But here is the truth: It's not a tricky thing. It's either the truth, or it is a lie. In business, gray is a dangerous color. Beyond the philosophical discussion is a tangible truth: If you lie to us, even once, we are gone. We will never trust you again—nor should we.

There are no white lies in business. In our personal relationships, perhaps. We can save someone's feelings as to why we were unable (or unwilling) to make it to a birthday party. You can tell a buddy that his belly looks fine in that shirt. You can lavish praise on the painful-to-watch fourth-grade school play and tell your ten-year-old that it was the best show you have ever seen!

In business, however, anything less than the truth shakes our confidence and makes us wary of anything you tell us afterward. To be clear, you can spare someone embarrassment when denying that person a job or save a vendor relationship by simply saying that you are going in a different direction on this project, but that's simply being tactful. That's showing sensitivity and merely omitting additional facts that might cause distress or hurt feelings. Being less than truthful for substantive matters is a different situation entirely.

Lying to customers when things go awry may buy you time until you can figure out a solution, but it will come back to bite you eventually. In business today, as it has always been, honesty matters. And lest you think this is an obvious admonition, consider the myriad ways that businesses are less than truthful:

If you are struggling to make a payment, don't pretend that your accounts payable person is out sick. We will be skeptical (and we can see their activity on social media). If a delivery is going to be late, don't tell us that the factory delayed the shipment unless it is true. When you are less than truthful, you may be saving face in the moment, but you are losing credibility in the long run.

There is no shortage of scenarios where things can go off the rails. It happens. We understand. However, when it affects us—when we are waiting for our merchandise, expecting a technician to arrive, making a financial commitment predicated on anticipated payment from you—we are less forgiving. Even in those stressful situations, honesty isn't just the best policy. It's the only acceptable policy.

Tell us the real reason why you are aging our payables, and tell us when you will make the payment—and keep your word. If a delivery is going to be late, tell us the truth as to why that is.

In George Orwell's classic dystopian classic *1984,* the government worked to keep order by hijacking both the conversation and the vernacular. They distracted from the truth by spinning not only the conversations, but the language as well. The Ministry of Peace was responsible for waging war; the Ministry of Truth disseminated propaganda; and the Firemen in the story burned books. When the company would announce changes in the factory quotas or provision allocation, the claimed increases were really decreases and simply counted on the people not noticing or commenting.

Today, we call that gaslighting. Its intentional manipulation that attempts to cause people to question their own memory with claims that what they know is not true and what they remember is flawed.

We see this in business when companies are disingenuous in presenting their "value" in the hopes that we don't notice. When they increase the price, then put the item "on sale" for a price fairly close or even above what it was and tell us we are getting a great deal, they hope we are too busy or distracted to notice. When they reduce the size of the portion but keep the container the same size and charge the same price, they assume we won't notice or care.

Some companies will use packaging requirements to fool us by posting their very low calories and healthy ingredients on the package, as required by law. It's only after closer inspection that we realize that the can of Coke is supposed to quench the thirst of 2 1/2 people, or the 250 calorie mac and cheese needs to be multiplied by 4. It's not an out-and-out lie, but make no mistake, it is an attempt to mislead or deceive.

When the airlines take away, food, blankets, free baggage, and more, but then turn around and pretend that buying back these amenities on an à la carte basis is giving us choices, we know it is merely spin. They increased (or regained) their profits by giving us less and then made even more by charging us for the items that they just took away. They call it smart business. We call it shady. We know that it's a tough marketplace for airlines, but your spin makes us less inclined to advocate for you.

I am not begrudging any company smart profits. As a business speaker and consultant, I am an unapologetic capitalist. Making money is not inherently evil. It pays bills, feeds families, diapers babies, and pays to heat homes. Just cut the spin. You're not that clever. We know what you are doing, and in most cases, we know why you are doing it.

Business is tough and you need to be smart about your expenditures. We get it. But you are losing credibility when you present it as anything other than what it is. If it walks like a duck and quacks like a duck. . . . Every time we roll our eyes at your words or your excuses, it is a reflection of lost respect and lost loyalty.

When your CEO goes on camera after yet another PR blunder claiming, "This is not who we are," we roll our eyes. It *is* who you are. That's why you keep having to go on TV to make excuses. We don't trust your spin. We have become cynical consumers, and for good reason.

"I'm calling to check on the payment for the January order. We talked early last week, and you told me that the payment would go out last Friday."

"Yeah. Sorry about that. The check run got held up because our bookkeeper was out. It'll be on next week's check run. So sorry for the miscommunication."

Sound familiar?

"Any word on the flight to Detroit?" we ask the gate agent. "The sign said it was delayed twenty minutes, but now it says an hour? Do you know what we should expect?"

"We were having mechanical issues with that plane."

"The other gate agent said it was weather on the East Coast."

C'mon! Get your stories straight.

When you say you love your loyal "premier" customers, yet make it increasingly harder each year for them to use the perks that they've earned, they feel mislead.

When you tell us that "Your call is very important to us," but you keep us on hold for forty-five minutes, we knows it's just talk.

We have become accustomed to inflated hotel room rates and deceptively priced airline tickets. Once they add all the resort charges, landing fees, and taxes, the real price can be far in excess of the quoted rate. Luring us in with a price that is not really the price is disingenuous.

Southwest Airlines has capitalized on the distrust and offers a more straightforward and honest view of their passenger costs. They have leveraged that into a legitimate competitive advantage and marketing campaign touting their "TransFarency." Brilliant.

Lest you think that good PR and spin are interchangeable, they are not. PR, done well and ethically, is simply the effective communication between a company and their various audiences. Good PR helps customers and others better understand what the company wants to communicate. Done well, it's clear, efficient, and effective.

Spin, on the other hand, is an intentional alteration of a scenario to maximize the perception that the communicator wants to impart. It can involve cherry-picking facts to only present those that are beneficial to the company or individual so as to create a false perception, or the most flattering version of their truth.

You will see this following a political debate as the "spin doctors" present the candidates' positive moments during exchanges, often ignoring moments that were more tenuous.

Confirmation bias will have the true believers, the most ardent fans, only hearing what they want or seeking messengers that will deliver their preconceived version of the truth. Polarization will have others distrusting everything they hear. We live in challenging times.

The best solution is opting for truth, transparency, and telling it like it is whenever you can. And most of the time, you can.

WHY YOU DO IT:

You lie or spin, hedge or omit, deceive or gaslight for a few basic reasons: You screwed up and want to shift blame (or an employee has done this); you are intentionally deceitful to maximize profits (misleading packaging or product claims); you are afraid of a difficult conversation that might arise from being entirely truthful (the most common reason); or you are simply a liar (I hope this is rare).

Most companies are less than honest because the truth makes them look bad. Either they'd rather not admit to the shortcomings of the product or the reason for underperformance, or they are unable or unwilling to do what they should. So, they make excuses. In either case, it's succumbing to a defensive primal instinct. The problem is that we have all been mislead or lied to so often that our BS meter is cranked up to maximum sensitivity.

WHY WE HATE IT:

It's more than the fact that we hate being lied to (we do). When your words are suspect, we run everything you say through our BS filter. So, even when you are being completely forthright, we tend to distrust.

Trust is at the heart of every relationship—business or personal. In intimate personal relationships, we are devastated when we discover deceit. In our business relationships, deceit or spin just makes us feel bad. Feeling bad doesn't portend a long and fruitful customer relationship. The two biggest offenses in a business relationship are deceit and underperformance. In the worst of all worlds, the two are linked.

A BETTER APPROACH:

Own it. Own your underperformance. Own your shortcomings. Be human and fall on your sword—just don't make the same mistake again. Make an organizational commitment to honesty and transparency. It doesn't go in a training binder on the shelf. It is an agenda item in your staff meetings. Create a list of likely scenarios that you and your team might face, and agree ahead of time how you will handle them.

Your customers will find your candor refreshing and your willingness to be straight with them attractive. In fact, like Southwest Airlines, you can use your candor as a differentiator in your marketplace.

7

We Don't Want to Do Business Your Way

A satisfied customer is the best business strategy of all.
–Michael LeBoeuf

Driving the business process improvement wave of the 1980s and the 1990s was a hyper-analysis of internal processes and the workflow of organizations: "If we are going to get better, reduce mistakes, streamline our manufacturing, increase revenue, and boost customer satisfaction, we have to do things differently," they said.

From Six Sigma, Kaizen, TQM (Total Quality Management), CQI (Continuous Quality Improvement), and other movements, organizations were admonished to dissect their processes and look at every point along the continuum to discover, or uncover areas for correction, standardization, mistake elimination, and quality improvement. It was suggested, and has been demonstrated, that an improved and predictable process flow will bring with it improved efficiency, work performance, job satisfaction, and profitability.

Somewhere along the line, it became accepted practice to design the external workflow with the same mindset as the internal: "If we can guide our customers along a consistent and predictable path through our buying and delivery process, then we can increase the likelihood that they will interact with us, search and buy the way we want them to." Note the operative words "the way we want them to."

What is lost in that calculus is the question: "How would our customers *prefer* to interact, search, shop, and buy from us?"

The CEO of a well-known mid-sized company reached out to my office after seeing me present at an industry conference in Las Vegas. The voicemail message he left at our office was a bit garbled, and my assistant was unable to decipher his phone number, although his name and his company were clearly audible. She visited the company website to try to retrieve his phone number, but there was none to be found. She searched for an email address, but once again, nothing. What she did find was a contact form. Yes, the dreaded website contact form.

Bypassing the form (as most will do), she was able to use Internet search mechanisms (tricks) learned from my brilliant speaker colleague Sam Richter (look him up!) and was able to find his contact information. We set up a call, and one of the first things I asked him was why they made it so difficult for people to contact company representatives.

"Oh, anyone can reach us," he said dismissively. "They just need to fill out the contact form."

"But what if they want to call or email you?" I inquired.

"Well, we would prefer that they use the form," he repeated.

"That's clear," I remarked. "Not that they have any other choice. But what if they want to call or email?" I repeated. "Why don't you include a phone number?"

This was his honest-to-God response:

"Well, if we include a phone number, people are going to call us."

"Who is going to call you?" I asked, disbelieving this conversation. "Your customers?"

"Oh, they will call all day long!" he says with exasperation in his voice.

"But isn't that telling you how they want to do business with you?" I asked calmly. "I mean, if the people who buy your products and pay your bills want to call you, then why don't you let them call you?"

Silence on the other end of the phone. "But too many phone calls take our staff off task," he says.

"Isn't working with customers and being responsive to clients the most important task of any organization?" I asked.

Needless to say, this began a fruitful business relationship between our companies.

Of course, the answers to those questions are complicated. Staffing, delineation of duties, process flow, cash flow, and other issues have to be considered, but the broader lesson is clear: When we drive customers to do business with us the way we want them to, they will do one of three things:

begrudgingly comply, work around your restrictions, or leave you in frustration.

To be clear, there are smart and welcome customer-centered processes that are good for everyone. Fast-casual restaurants design the line (queue) to expedite entree selection, customize meals with options, and receive payment in a way that makes the line move quickly. It works—for everyone. Ikea has redefined the customer experience and takes people on a brilliantly designed path/journey through the rooms of our homes and areas of our lives, only to end up with an easy way to load up and purchase all that we have selected.

The challenge comes when you design your business and the customer experience to accommodate you and your team with insufficient consideration of your customers. When you restrict client freedom or choice, and create policies so that your people have to work less hard, you are serving your team at the expense of your customer. And remember, the customer isn't just king or queen, he or she is prince, duke, third earl of something . . . you get the picture.

This is not about the customer always being right. It's about being careful to ensure that your approach is not wrong. If you are dismissing what they may want in favor of what your team prefers, you are missing the mark. Don't cater to your team. Treat your team very, very well, but cater to your customers. This may sound harsh, but your team doesn't pay the bills. *They are the bills.*

I was speaking at an international conference and a large group of us went out to dinner together. They had made arrangements for us to dine at a cool restaurant in a remodeled factory near the harbor. It was very large, and the dining room was expansive. The hostess led our group of fifteen people to four tables situated near each other and placed menus on each table.

We stood looking at each other for a moment wondering who should sit with whom and instead simply started pushing the tables together to create a long table where we could all sit together. The waiter rushed over and started pulling the tables apart shaking his head.

"You cannot move the tables!" he said rather harshly.

"We'd like to sit together, please," a member of our group said. The place was not crowded, and she apologized to him but noted that there were fifteen of us, and we didn't want to be split up.

"We can't allow that," he reiterated. "It's just a big hassle to drag the tables back and reset them afterward," he added with a condescending "so sorry" expression on his face.

So, we left and went across the street to a different restaurant. As we headed for the exit, we noticed that the restaurant was half empty, but it sure looked pretty and the tables were in their proper place. They wanted to do business their way; we wanted it our way. The convenience of their staff took precedence over the desires of their customers. It was more important for them to not have to reset tables than let a party of fifteen sit wherever they wanted. Insane!

The request wasn't unreasonable. They were unreasonable! In that rustic old factory dining room, they won the battle, but lost the war.

A gymnastic, dance, and cheer academy was doing great work with kids. The budding gymnasts and dancers were learning, engaged, and often making great progress. The young instructors were qualified, enthusiastic, and loved working with the kids. The problem was that the academy was struggling with retention. When the session ended and it came time to re-enroll for the next-level classes, the parents of the kids in the program too often opted out. Why?

I was asked to come in, look at the business, audit some classes, talk to the parents, interview the staff, and help diagnose the problem.

So, I arrived late on a Tuesday afternoon. As I walked through the front doors, I knew in a matter of seconds what the problem was, and the reasons for the exodus became quickly apparent. Signs, some printed and others handwritten, littered the walls of the facility and in particular, the parents' waiting area.

Signs were everywhere warning of all the things the parents were NOT to do. *"No talking to your children during class." "No eating in the viewing area." "We are not a babysitting service! Parents of kids who are not picked up within 15 minutes of class ending will be billed $25." "Missed classes would not be reimbursed without 48 hours notice."* On and on.

I asked the center director to explain the signs.

"Oh, those are for the parents," he said, brushing the question off.

"I can tell that," I said. "But what's the purpose?"

"We need to teach the parents . . ." he began before I cut him off.

"Wait," I said. "I thought you were supposed to be teaching the kids."

"Well yeah, but . . ." his voice trailed off.

"Why are you imposing fines on the parents who get here late? Sometimes parents are running late. It's not like the kids are waiting in the rain. They are watching TV in the lobby or playing on their cell phones," I remarked. "Who cares if a kid sits for fifteen minutes?"

"It's really an issue of respect," he said.

"I agree!" I said. "Why are you disrespecting your busy parents who are working hard and entrusting their children to you and trying to get here on time after work, or making dinner or buying groceries while the kids are dancing or tumbling? Is it respectful to scold adults who are paying you lots of money, but who may be running late?"

He had no answers.

"Tell me about the signs that say: 'No popcorn in the viewing area,'" I asked.

"Oh, it makes a big mess and the staff has to clean it up," he says.

"Okay?" I ask. "And?" Silence. "Let's be clear," I continued. "You have a popcorn machine."

"Yes," he responded.

"You sell popcorn to the parents," I continued. "They like popcorn and buy it from you, but they are not allowed to eat the popcorn that you just sold them," I said, not attempting to hide the irony.

"Well, they can eat it, just not in the viewing area," he said.

"But that's where the parents want to be so they can watch their kids!" I said, stating the obvious. "Who are you serving here? The employees or your paying customers?"

The things that made life easier for the staff clearly took precedent over the things that served their customers. The kids were having lots of fun, but the parents certainly were not—*and they were the ones writing the checks!* (Or in this case, deciding to no longer write checks.)

Long story short, the signs came down. All of them. Snacks were allowed everywhere except on the gym floor. The staff vacuuming twice a day was part of their duties and the price they paid for selling popcorn, pizza, and more. Penalties were eliminated. Scolding of parents stopped, and restrictions that didn't directly affect the kids' learning or safety were eliminated. What was always a welcoming and nurturing place for the kids finally became one for the parents as well. Needless to say, reenrollment rose.

When you overtly, or even subtly, push us to do business with you the way you want us to, we get frustrated and often leave. When you offer self-checkout lanes, but intentionally understaff the traditional checkout lanes because *you* want us to do it ourselves, we get frustrated at the lack of choice. When we ask to be seated in the open front section of your restaurant, but you tell us that it is a particular server's turn and we need to go to the back dining room, we are made to feel uncomfortable.

In short, we are always learning better ways to conduct business. Continuous improvement should be continuous. However, be careful that your new process is one that doesn't make it easier for you but harder for us. You have every right to decide how you want us to contact you, interact with you, and buy from you, but don't forget that we get to decide if we want to play along.

WHY YOU DO IT:

Your business processes, both internal and external, were designed they way they were for a reason. You are working to make things better, solve problems, shorten wait times, increase efficiency and predictability, address staff and customer complaints, and more. But too often, you fail to revisit past decisions to see if they are still valid and smart.

I'd be willing to bet that you don't even know when or why some decisions were made, yet you still adhere to them and go to work each day with the understanding that this is the way you do it. Nobody sets out to annoy or inconvenience their customers and prospects, but it happens over time.

WHY WE HATE IT:

Kids say it best: "You're not the boss of me!" We know what we want, when we want it, and generally, how we want it. It doesn't mean that everyone is unreasonable. Quite the contrary, we will follow your process and path when it makes sense—and it most often does. When it doesn't, or it is inconvenient, or it makes us wait, we begin to look for alternatives.

A BETTER APPROACH:

The better approach is to ask if there is a better approach. Keep asking. Often, you will not know a problem exists until it is brought to your attention. Don't wait for the complaint. (But don't ignore the complaints either.) Go through your customer's journey with fresh eyes. Ask people who are representative of your ideal customer to go through your process. What did they like? What did they find frustrating, inconvenient, confusing, or arduous? Put together a task force or consumer panel. Ask them: If you could wave a magic wand and create the perfect customer journey through our company or our industry, starting from scratch, what would that perfect path look like? And then listen to the answer.

8

Don't Punish Everyone for the Actions of a Few

What loneliness is more lonely than distrust?
–George Eliot

When I turned sixteen years old, I earned my drivers license and with it, a new level of freedom. I could go wherever I wanted, whenever I wanted, keeping in mind the reasonable restrictions from my father. One Saturday morning that very same week, my dad came into my bedroom as I was waking up and sat down on the edge of my bed. We proceeded to have a conversation that proved to be profound in my life.

"David," he began. "You are now sixteen years old. You are not a man yet by any stretch, so don't get cocky," he added with a smile. "But you are old enough to make your own decisions. I'm a single dad with six kids, and it's hard enough keeping track of your younger brothers and sister. So, here's the deal," he said. "You no longer have a curfew. You can stay with your friends or stay up all night. That's up to you. But you still have to make it to school every day, keep your grades up, and do your chores. If you are going to stay at a buddy's house, just let me know where you are so I don't worry."

Then he said the one sentence that spoke to my heart, my conscience, and my moral center: "I will trust you until you prove untrustworthy." I knew what would happen if I violated his trust. I knew the reapplications of restrictions. I knew the disappointment I would cause, and I knew that earning back that trust would take a very long time.

As a sixteen-year-old young man, I was afforded a level of respect from a man I respected greatly. He said in no uncertain terms: "I am not expecting that you are going to disappointment me. To the contrary, I expect that you will make me proud. I expect you to do the right thing, make good choices, and live up to my opinion of you." His confidence lifted me up and made me want to be a good person, and prove to him that he was right to trust me.

What do you expect of your customers and clients? Do you expect that they will be honest, good citizens and shoot straight with you? Or do you expect that they will shoplift, fraudulently return items, and file false claims? Some will, to be sure; but how many, really?

Before you get up in arms quoting statistics of what fraud and theft cost your industry each year, please know that nobody is arguing that. As business owners, it is crucial that we safeguard our products and process against those who would do us harm. This chapter is about the effect of your suspicion and safeguards on the vast majority who would not, and never will. Like the police officers who patrol our neighborhoods, we have to balance the need to protect with the obligation to serve.

When you implement protectionist policies to guard against the 1 percent who might take advantage or try to cheat you, you are too often offending the 99 percent who never would. When companies want to verify our personal information prior to making a purchase, we know that it is for our protection. But why do some want to verify our purchases *after* we make the purchase? That's just checking to make sure we didn't steal anything. The first one we understand. The second one we don't.

We are expected to stand in a line with our shopping cart at Sam's Club or Costco *after* we paid for our items, so a very nice retiree can visually scan our basket and compare it to our receipt. They are checking to make sure we aren't stealing anything. Regardless of the friendly banter or the smiley face they draw on our receipt, their purpose is clear: They are there to check if their paying customers are leaving with items they didn't pay for. Insulting. A minor inconvenience to be sure, but insulting nonetheless.

The police have to show probable cause to search us. Ernie, the engaging grandpa, is positioned near the exit of Costco to look for forty-year-old working mom shoplifters. Really? I just spent hundreds of dollars buying absurdly large jugs of mayonnaise, off-brand jeans, restaurant-style warming pans, eighty rolls of toilet paper, and enough ibuprofen to last a decade! I just went through the checkout lane and paid for my items ten yards away and pushed my cart straight toward the exit. Are you really worried that I stole something?

Of course, I don't give them a hard time as they are just doing their jobs, but I would prefer to not stand in another line and just take my items straight to my car.

We understand reasonable measures that companies take to reduce theft and keep costs down, but when did we start treating everyone like potential criminals or vandals? That dragnet isn't just catching bad players. It's catching primarily good people, and those good people (paying customers) are the only reason you are profitable.

I was walking around a clothing store outside of Kansas City and felt uncomfortable the entire time I was in the store (and not merely because 90 percent of the clothes were entirely inappropriate for my fifty-five-year-old body). From the moment I walked through the doors, I felt under surveillance—*because I was.* In fact, everyone was. In addition to the plain-clothed security personnel pretending to shop but watching my every move, the signs were hard to miss—everywhere, threatening to prosecute shoplifters. The dressing rooms were not only being monitored (yuck), but I also wasn't allowed to bring more than three items in with me—and absolutely no shoes!

"How many items?" the young woman asked me as I walked into the dressing room.

"I have four shirts, two pants, and a pair of shoes," I answered.

"You can only bring three items in with you, and no shoes allowed in the dressing rooms," she rattled off for probably the twenty-eighth time that day.

"But I would like to try on all of these items and see if the shoes fit," I said as nicely as I felt inclined to be.

"Nope," she said, smacking her gum. "Three, max. You can hang the other ones up out here. Try on the other items, and then bring the others back out, and I will let you take the other items back. And you can sit out here and try on the shoes."

Was she just doing her job and saying exactly what she was told to say? Yep. Absolutely. But someone told her to say that. Someone made a decision that it didn't matter how old someone was, how they were dressed, or what time it was. They were going to make it very, very difficult for anyone to steal from them!

They seemed much more concerned about what they would lose rather than what they might actually sell! What is lost in this dynamic is the customer who knows they have choices. Those with financial means simply won't stand for this. They will leave and take their dollars with them. The ones left are those who may not have the means. They may not have transportation or the ability to shop elsewhere.

Do not make this a racial or prejudicial issue! I certainly am not. I'm not suggesting for a minute that someone who looks like they have money should have different rules. The fact is that everyone—at every socioeconomic level— deserves respect. Everyone! They deserve to not be treated like criminals. Take reasonable precautions to prevent theft, but treat your customers—all of your customers—like human beings. Treat them like your business depends on it, because it does!

And while company losses from shoplifting, missing goods, cash shortages, and so on are approaching forty-five billion dollars[1] annually in America, statistics clearly show that employee theft accounts for a full 43 percent of those company losses.[2] Nearly half of these crimes are perpetrated by employees! So that young lady who wouldn't let me take more than three items into the dressing room was just as likely to stash merchandise out behind the dumpster for later retrieval.

Even if you are effective at reducing theft, what you are missing is the lost sales and customers as a result of your restrictive and offensive posture. You have no idea how many customers you have lost. You have no idea how many sales and future sales that walked out the door because your prospect opted out. Your expenses may be reduced, but I guarantee your revenue has declined as well. Reasonable trade-off? I'm not so sure.

Once again, I am not Pollyannish about the threats facing business owners, but I am sensitive to being painted with a broad brush. Your customers don't want to be treated like potential criminals with a cloud of distrust hanging over them. Nobody does. And what I experienced pales in comparison to the day-to-day reality of how minorities are treated by businesses and their employees. It is beyond offensive. It's tragic.

I called an Italian restaurant with a $600 catering order for a dinner party at my home. After ordering an absurd amount of food for my absurdly large family, I tried to pay with a credit card, but they wouldn't take a credit card over the phone.

"You need to show us the credit card when you come to pick it up," the restaurant worker said to me.

"But I am not the one picking it up," I responded. "My brother is going to pick it up tomorrow afternoon and bring it over."

"Then he will need to put it on his card," he replied.

"But I don't want my brother to pay for all this food. I am paying for it," I said.

"Then you will need to come and pick it up," he said.

"But I am fifteen miles away and I'll be preparing for the party, and he lives right there near you. I would like to pay for it now and have him come and pick it up tomorrow," I said, a bit exasperated. "I will gladly pay for it right now. Just go ahead and run my credit card."

"I'm sorry, but you can come in today and bring your credit card," he said, as if he had thought of a good idea.

"I can't make it there. I'm working. That's why I am ordering over the phone the day before. This is a $600 order, and I'm not allowed to pay for it ahead of time?"

"Not without seeing the card. Sorry."

Sigh. "Just cancel the order. I will order from someone else," I said.

"Um . . . let me talk to my manager," he said. Two minutes later: "Okay. We can do it, but just this time."

Right answer. But the truth is they should also do it next time and the next time—for everyone.

They were so worried about not being "taken" that they were going to walk away from a $600 order—or let me walk away. They made things difficult for their customers who were choosing them over all the other options for expensive takeout catering. Crazy! Of course they should protect themselves, but they could have simply ensured that payment cleared before the customer took the food. Simple solution.

"Thanks for calling XYZ Corporation. Be advised that this call is being recorded, so we have proof if you try to lie about something later on."

Business has changed, and trust and respect have fallen by the wayside. At the end of the day, don't we want our customers to feel welcomed and appreciated, and to enjoy doing business with us?

WHY YOU DO IT:

Most protective policies are enacted as a result of being burned. Someone used a stolen credit card, so you restrict cards where you can't verify the identity. People have shoplifted, so you make it clear that you will prosecute shoplifters. You want to avoid he said/she said, so you record our conversations. You want to avoid kids' chocolate-covered fingers touching your racks of blouses, so you say no food or drink in the store. I get it, but your honest customers don't really like it. Just sayin'.

WHY WE HATE IT:

We aren't going to steal from you, lie to you, or file a lawsuit against you. Some will to be sure, but we aren't them. How do you know? You don't. But you don't know that your kids' friends aren't criminals or your neighbors aren't going to sue you either. And you don't treat them with suspicion. You treat them like friends and neighbors. You can say those signs aren't directed at us, but it feels like they're directed at everyone. When we come to spend our money with you, at the very least, we expect you to be grateful and to treat us kindly and with respect—and not as potential criminals.

A BETTER APPROACH:

Trust people until they prove untrustworthy. Better yet—trust, but verify. Simple verification mechanisms will solve most of your theft and fraud issues. Requiring a receipt for a cash refund is reasonable. Otherwise, let them exchange. Close off the path between the register and the exit so you know everyone leaving has already paid. Count the items going in and out of the dressing room—even if it's more than three. Geez! Verify payment before items or services are rendered. Don't follow us around and peer at us over racks of clothing to make sure we don't steal things. Just have cameras. We are cool with that. And finally, treat your employees the same way. The honest ones will have nothing to fear.

People understand reasonable verification to protect your business, but they don't appreciate suspicion while shopping. It's disrespectful and largely unnecessary. Don't treat your customers like a problem waiting to happen. Treat us like customers ready to buy. You'll make a lot more money. Promise.

9

Fix Your Dysfunctional Website

Store windows are like landing pages on the website.
–Angela Ahrendts

As of this writing, there are nearly two billion websites on the Internet. Yours is just one of them. One of (say it slowly) two B I L L I O N.

In the early days of the Web, simply being there with your online, backlit brochure was a competitive advantage. Then, it became an issue of who had the flashiest website with intro animation and lots of bells and whistles. Today, the Web winners offer attractive, stripped-down, easy-to-navigate online resources. You can buy or find what you are looking for quickly and easily. The most visited website today is Google. How complicated is their home page?

The problem is that people don't follow best practices; they follow their gut. Most businesses have websites that try to replicate what they might put in an advertisement or a brochure. Often, even their content-rich and highly functional websites are so overburdened and complex that they inadvertently drive customers away because things are just too hard to find.

Companies have no idea how many prospects they are losing because of a poor online experience—though a quick perusal of their Web analytics might give them a meaningful snapshot. On the other hand, some offenses are quite intentional in their delivery, though not necessarily in their effect.

Pop-ups and pop-unders are designed to make sure that you don't leave without providing your contact information. We don't like them; they don't care.

Contact forms are designed to capture your information and reach out to them in their way. We want to call or email. They don't care.

They promise to provide the information we seek if we will simply click their button to receive it. We are then redirected instead to where they want us to go on the customer path, and not where we thought we were going. It's an all too common website bait and switch.

My sweetheart Laurel and I were looking for some land in the mountains outside our home near Denver, Colorado. We have always wanted a mountain retreat and decided that a cabin in the woods would offer a nice respite for our family and from my frequent travels for work.

On an autumn Saturday morning, Laurel and I drove up to an area less than an hour away from our home and found a few good options. We wanted a plot big enough to expand in later years and build a compound of buildings; a bunkhouse for the grandkids, man-cave/shop for me, a place where my brother and his family could build a home, and more. It's fun to dream a little.

When we got home that night, we decided to go online and look at companies that design and build log homes. After perusing multiple websites, we found a very cool log home company. Great designs, lots of pictures, and a multitude of options. Not only did they sell log cabin kits, they even offered an option to fly out their team to do the actual construction. When we found a model that we really liked, I click on the button that said "Click here for pricing."

Do you think they provided a price? Of course not! The button took us to a contact form. So frustrating! Revise that: infuriating! There was no way to get the price of something they were trying to sell unless I filled out their form. They were clearly worried that the price would scare us away, but instead, *they* drove us away. I wanted the price, and they didn't want to give it to me unless I jumped through their hoops. I wasn't playing their game.

Remember, the primary challenge of any marketing program is to get a prospect to directly connect with you and your products or services. If we can get an audience, we have a good shot at converting that prospect into a customer. Connection can be done in four primary ways:

1. Get them to come to your location.
2. Meet face to face offsite at their location, over coffee, and so on.
3. Connect with them over the phone or video chat.
4. Get them to your website.

If you are able to elicit any of these pre-buying behaviors from a prospect, you have won the initial battle. We should be able to convert the lion's share of prospects we can get in front of. Getting someone to visit your website to actually inquire about price is a huge win. These are hard-won victories in the battle for customers and not to be squandered.

The one thing you don't want to do with that qualified, interested prospect—*the one thing* you don't want to do—is anger or frustrate them. That is exactly what this log home company did to me and does to others.

To be clear, I was inquiring about the price of a very expensive product—a new home—and they misled me, frustrated me, and destroyed any good feelings I had about the company. Once again, they had me right there where they wanted me, and then they pissed me off. Ludicrous!

I'm not naïve about their thinking. The reasons for the redirect are perfectly clear: They want to get me on the phone so they can ascertain my needs, prequalify me, suggest options that might better suit my needs, tailor a package to thrill me, and capture my contact information so they can stay in touch. I get it. I guarantee you that is the exact conversation their sales team had during their website development meeting.

There is one problem, however. The button said "Click here for pricing." They lied. The page could have said, for example: "Price range: $220,000 to $280,000 depending on building materials, options, and upgrades. We would be happy to schedule a very brief conversation to explain how our beautiful, affordable homes are priced and can be tailored to fit your family and your dreams. (We have some very cool options available!) Click here to tell us the best way to reach you, and a design specialist will get back to you at the time of your choosing."

I know there are some of you who would not have a major issue with the website page redirection. I'm not implying everyone has the same gut reaction that I do. But enough people would that they are likely losing millions of dollars every year from prospects who simply left frustrated. And they have no idea this is happening!

Of course, the most frustrating website offense is the lack of contact information, or hard-to-find contact information. Hell, hard-to-find anything is frustrating. Being hard to reach is addressed throughout this book because it is so prevalent in business today.

Gone are the days of grabbing the massive phone book and searching through the thousands of pages while humming the alphabet song to find you and scan for your phone number. We expect to be able to find contact information quickly and easily. Are we spoiled? My response will always be the same: Yes. And? The expectation is what it is regardless of your thoughts on where society and technology has led us.

If your content-rich, fifteen-layers-deep, multiple drop-down menu, Flash-driven, hard-to-spell website makes it hard to find you and hard to find what we are looking for, you will lose us. Unless you are a single-source provider, we will simply click away—because we can.

The problem is that you know your own website far too well. If we were sitting across from you and mentioned that we couldn't find something, you could open your laptop and show us very quickly where to find it.

"Look. It's very simple," you would tell us. "Go to the home page and scroll down to where it says 'Locations.' Click that, and then you can choose your state. On your state, if you put in your zip code over here on the right, it will show you a list of all the locations within twenty miles. Click each location to open its own home page. Isn't that cool? So, once you are on the home page, you can click to see the staff, the items, all the options, and where to click for more information and even how to order. Here is the link to the Frequently Asked Questions so you don't even have to call. Just scroll down to find your issue. It's all right here. If you log in with your password, it will take you right to your past orders, and you can set your own preferences."

Honestly, how the hell was I supposed to know all of that? Do you really think your customers are going to spend forty-five minutes figuring out how to navigate your "robust" website? They were gone after "Click away from the home page!"

Admittedly, it probably took your team months to create this hearty website, replete with everything we could ever want to know and ask. The point is that your website shouldn't be designed to provide everything that someone might want to know and ask. It should help your prospects find what they need or want, so they can learn about you, contact you, or buy from you easily and quickly. It doesn't have to do everything, just the things they need to do in order get them where they want to go.

Millions of sales are lost every day because people click away from confusing websites. How long do you stay on a website when you don't quickly find what you want? Not very long. Nobody does.

The fact is, there are companies that are very good at this—and I'm not talking about Web design companies trying to get your business. I mean retailers, consulting firms, universities, restaurants, ride-share companies, and more. There are awesome, functional sites everywhere. Look them up. (I'm not going to list any because this book will quickly become antiquated as things change so quickly.)

Of course, there are also billions of antiquated, cumbersome, and incomplete websites as well. Keep in mind that if you haven't updated your website in two years, it is likely very outdated. Others recommend every year to eighteen months, though that can be cost prohibitive.

In reality, it shouldn't cost any more to build an attractive and effective website than it does to build a crappy one. There are plenty of Web developers who will disagree, but think about this: There are millions of talented people around the world who do great work for a fair fee. Of course, what is fair in India is vastly different than what is fair in Chicago. You work with whomever you wish, but the fact is that options are out there at every price point. Resources like Upwork.com, Fiverr.com, 99designs.com, and others give access to millions of talented professionals around the world.

Whomever you choose to work with, know that the size of a computer screen doesn't change based on how much you pay. A website will fill up your computer screen from the upper left corner to the lower right. What you choose to put in that space—what you tolerate from your Web developer—is entirely up to you. Be demanding, and make sure that your website doesn't just look good, but is also astonishingly easy for your customers to access and navigate. Most customers will check you out online before they contact you. They must like what they see, or you will never see them again.

And if you make the conscious choice to omit direct contact information from your website, then you might as well just close this book right now and start preparing for your going out of business sale. The rest of the subjects covered in this book won't matter much if you're out of business.

WHY YOU DO IT:

Websites are dysfunctional largely because people don't recognize what a functional website is and how crucial it is to the success of your business. Anything that delays, confuses, or frustrates your customers will drive them away from your site and into the arms of your competitors.

The other issue is that you're likely too close to your own website. It's not that you are emotionally invested, it's that you are far too familiar with it's functionality and navigation. You know where everything is and can easily navigate it. Your customers don't know it and often won't take the time to learn it.

WHY WE HATE IT:

The primary reason we hate this is that we have become accustomed to getting information quickly and easily. You may not think that your website is complicated, but you made it! You live with it everyday. We, on the other hand, are probably navigating it for the first time!

If you can't (or won't) give us an answer or access to a real person, we will just find someone who will. If the navigation is confusing, we just leave, and if there is too much information, we won't search through endless dropdown menus and multiple pages to find what we want.

A BETTER APPROACH:

Simplicity. Make your value proposition front and center. Don't make us figure out what you do or how to reach you. Good websites have headlines that tell us who you are, what you do, and who you do it for. If we have to click more than twice to find anything or anyone, then the third click will be to click away.

Gather your team and ask: What are the top five things that prospects and customers come to our website looking for? Make sure those things are front and center and easy to find. Do an audit of your top three competitors' websites. What do they do well? Where do they fall short? Remember that the vast majority of prospects will check you out online before ever calling or visiting. Make sure they like what they see.

10

You Get One Chance, So Don't Blow It

If somebody is gracious enough to give me a
second chance, I won't need a third.
–Pete Rose

One of the biggest casualties of the widespread dynamic of broken customer experience is the death of the second chance.

In yesteryear, if we had a bad experience, we might come back to a vendor, store, or restaurant to see if things would be better the next time around. We would simply try a different menu item, or trust that we would encounter a different person on the other end of the phone. But in this age of an astonishing array of choices and widespread quality, it's almost always easier to just choose an alternative rather than take a chance on a second bad experience.

We reject the second chance for two reasons. First, simply out of fear (expectation) that the second experience won't be any better than the first—especially if the first bad one really put us in a bind—like someone didn't follow through, or we were embarrassed in front of a friend or client. The other reason why we don't often give second chances in business is more personal. We don't like feeling slighted, mistreated, or ripped-off. We take it personally, as if we were disrespected, and we don't respond well to disrespect. We paid and didn't get what we asked for. We made an appointment, and you didn't show up.

Despite our brushing it off or telling you not to worry about it when you apologize, we aren't okay with it. Declining to offer a second chance may not be out of fear, but simply out of a belief that you don't deserve a second chance. You let me down, and I refuse to reward that behavior.

Of course, this may sound a little petty and not very understanding, but the truth is that people can be petty and not very understanding! It's the reality of today's fast-paced, hustle-bustle, do-or-die world. If customers feel disrespected, they don't want to return respect that they feel was unearned. I'm not referring to what should be, but what is, in regard to business options.

We simply don't tolerate poor service or a poor experience today. In a 2016 global consumer survey, 47 percent of those responding said they would take their business to a competitor within a day of receiving poor customer service, and 79 percent said they would do it that same week.[1]

I spent two months planning a really nice birthday for my wife. I had interviewed a few personal chefs over the phone and finally hired one to come to our home and prepare a wonderful spread for all the guests at a dinner party held in her honor. As a side note, I was also hosting a business gathering the following week and had secured the same personal chef to cover that event as well.

In the weeks prior to her birthday, the chef and I had multiple conversations, settled on the menu, and ensured gluten-free options to accommodate her dietary restrictions. I turned my attention to contacting the guests, getting the house cleaned, and other logistical issues.

On the Saturday morning of the event, I received a text message at 10:00 a.m. from the personal chef:

"I'm so sorry, but I am stuck in Kansas City and won't be able to make it tonight. We drove here to get a camper fixed and it won't be done until Monday. Sorry."

Uh, excuse me? My blood pressure started to boil, and I texted back. "What are you talking about? I gave you a deposit. We've been planning this for weeks. The event is tonight!"

"I know," she texted back. "I thought we would be back in time. I feel really bad about this." And here is the kicker: "But I will definitely be there for the Thursday event." (Um, no, you won't!)

I was furious as I scrambled to come up with an alternative for the event, weeks in the planning, but now only seven hours away! I called every personal chef within fifty miles and none were available or willing to take on this challenge with such short notice. In the end, with no other choices, I found a local restaurant and ordered pans of food from there.

It was fine, but I wanted more than fine. I planned ahead to make it great. I was willing to pay for great.

After a few hours, I had calmed down enough to send a follow-up text, and here is what I said:

I know you are just starting out in business, so let me give you some unsolicited advice.

I planned far ahead of the date and found an enthusiastic vendor who could meet my needs. When I pay your deposit, we have a contract. I have an expectation that you will do whatever it takes to honor your obligation.

When I'm on the other side and I am the vendor, I have two options: Do everything I can to fulfill my obligations, or find an alternative vendor who can take my place if something occurs. Your mindset should be: "How do I get back to Denver on a one-way flight to honor my obligation?" Even if I knew I would not make any money on the deal, I would work hard to get there if I ever expected to get additional work. The other option would be to say: "Sorry, I physically can't make it there, but I have called three of my colleagues in the industry who would be able to handle this for me so that your event will be successful."

What I got from you instead was "Sorry, I can't make it, but I will be there on Thursday." You made zero effort to find an alternative or make this right. You made zero effort to get back to Denver and honor your word. You left me out to dry and threw up your hands as if there was nothing you could do. But there was. You simply chose not to do it.

You do realize that I cannot trust you again and risk being burned, as I have twenty people flying in later this week for a business retreat. I will find another chef. This is an important lesson in business as you embark on your career. When you have an agreement, you do everything you can to honor it, or you backfill with other options.

Unforeseen things can always happen. It can happen to any of us. It's what you do to make it right that makes you a good business person. Best of luck to you.

If you fail to honor your word, we will most often not give you a second chance. Why? Because we don't want to and we don't have to. If you don't show up when you said you would, we write you off. When you promise a delicious meal and fail to deliver, we move on. When you promise big results and then underdeliver, we will try someone else. There are countless competitors standing in line to meet our needs. We're not being unkind or even trying to punish you. We just write you off. We're just very cognizant of the competitive marketplace and all the options at our disposal.

Then again, if you go beyond merely underdelivering to the point of angering or offending us, we will actively work against you. Gone are the days of the powerless consumer, relegated to ranting to his or her family and neighbors about how he or she was wronged. Today, people will use all the tools at their disposal (and there are many) to exact revenge through online rants and bad reviews. Delivering on your promises is more important today than ever before.

The fact is that things can and do go wrong, and it is often an issue of how it is handled that will determine if we will forgive (though we never forget).

In Web development, the term "minimum viable product" (MVP) is an important concept for clients who want Web functionality, but lack the initial funds needed to develop a robust menu of website capabilities. In other words, how cheap can I get basic functionality so the website works for my customers without spending a fortune on all the bells and whistles? The website can still look great, but they are only getting the basics.

In business, we can often run the risk of providing or delivering the MVP, or just what the client or customer is asking for and nothing more. This isn't about meeting their expectations, but feeling like the transaction alone is sufficient to sustain the relationship. If they ask for something and we give it to them, then we've done our job, right? Not necessarily. If we merely satisfy our customers, we are vulnerable to others who are intent on pleasing them, thrilling them, and knocking their socks off.

Your job in business is not merely to meet the *needs* of your customers, but also to satisfy their *wants*. The one chance you will likely get is your opportunity to please them to such an extent that it's an initial experience they are eager to repeat. Blowing it isn't necessarily caused by committing some offense, but can be a result of merely being forgettable.

"How was your experience working with so and so?"

"Fine."

Fine? Fine doesn't do it. Not today. When there are choices, "fine" gets left behind. "Really good" gets a repeat visit. "Terrific" gets a referral to a friend. And "unbelievable!" gets shared with thousands on review sites and over social media.

In most scenarios, you get one chance before customers move on. Look at every point of contact along your customer's path and ensure that it exceeds "fine." Ask your team. Ask your customers what they would *love*, and try to deliver it.

Train your people to read your customers. Dissatisfaction is pretty easy to recognize. If a diner has left 90 percent of a meal uneaten, ask: "Was something wrong with your meal? Or "Did you not like your selection? I'd be happy to have the kitchen make you something else. Honestly, no charge!" If your consulting client is less communicative than in prior weeks, reach out. If a project comes back without achieving the results your promised, address it head-on and make it right.

Remember, most dissatisfied customers won't complain; they just won't come back. Not only do we have to work hard to ensure that we meet our customers' expectations, we have to find ways of discovering dissatisfaction before it results in an exodus. The job of your people is not to merely facilitate transactions. They have to meet and exceed the exceptions of your customers by delivering excellence. Their job is to not to babysit your business, but to build it.

There is an important distinction between facilitating a transaction and delivering excellence. Too many think their job is to find an item for a customer, ring up a transaction, deliver food, build a home, clean a carpet, hook up your Wi-Fi, calculate your taxes, or manufacture a part. The problem is that anyone and everyone in your space can do that. If that's all you do, even if you do it extraordinary well, you run the risk of someone else doing it better, faster, cheaper, more memorably, friendlier, or with additional amenities. The one chance you get is not to merely avoid blowing it, but to avoid merely delivering it.

WHY YOU DO IT:

Too often, the focus of the organization is on sales and customer acquisition, rather than the delivery of the services itself. I'm not suggesting that you don't recognize the importance of outstanding delivery, but we all get caught up in the customer acquisition part off the continuum. It's what happens after we seal the deal that determines whether or not we hold onto that customer.

WHY WE HATE IT:

Whether you know it or not, every time we engage with you, reach out, or buy from you, it is an audition of sorts. We aren't baiting you, but we are trying you out—even if we've tried you before. If you disappoint us, then we will likely look elsewhere. If you offend us, or we feel violated, we will actively work against you to seek satisfaction through bad online reviews and poor word of mouth. When we take a chance and give you our money or our time, don't blow it.

A BETTER APPROACH:

Someone has to be accountable for managing the successful and enjoyable delivery of your products and services, ensuring both customer retention and frequency of purchase. We will always have someone overseeing sales, but it's often a bit amorphous as to who is overseeing the delivery.

Even in my speaking business, the "business" is getting the gig, even though I know that I couldn't build a sustainable business if I don't also hit it out of the park on stage. Customer experience isn't just about a pleasant sales experience, but also about being hyperfocused on the successful delivery and follow-up.

Imagine that every customer is a first-time customer. What would you do to engage with them, ask if their needs were met, check back with them, and follow up? We all know the vast cost differential between recruitment and retention. Imaging this is your one chance to make a big impression—because it probably is.

11

It's Not What You Want to Say, It's What We Want to Hear

Don't make this life about you.
It's about other people.
–Kimberly Guilfoyle

One of the leading causes of business failure is passion. Here me out. "Follow your passion!" We have heard this for a generation from personal development "gurus" and schoolteachers, to parents, friends, and even celebrities, that fulfillment comes, we are told, from pursuing your dreams. "Follow your dreams, and you'll never work a day in your life!" the Internet meme screams out at us. Heeding this popular admonition has contributed to more business failures and personal financial struggles than almost any other flawed career advice.

"What's wrong with passion?" you ask. There is nothing wrong with passion, as long as there is a solid business model behind it. Alas, for most, there is not. That burning need you have to share your story, advocate for your cause, turn the world vegan, save the environment, or overcome your troubled past has nothing whatsoever to do with the reasons that most people want to buy.

If your message is focused on what you want to say, rather than what your customers want to hear, you're losing them.

This isn't a capitalist manifesto. It's a wakeup call that the rest of the world feels no obligation to help you live your dream and connect with your purpose. The world needs to feed their families, pay their bills, and invest in their future. We might want to buy your products, but few of us are willing to suffer through why you got into business and the cause you are promoting. It's not that its unimportant, it's just not relevant to us or why we are buying.

It is certainly en vogue to assert that customers need to know your "why." Yuck. Terrible advice. They aren't against your why, they just don't care. You may have a deep belief in some charitable cause helping villagers overseas, but she just likes that handbag and thinks it would look adorable with the new boots she just bought. The story might be interesting and even inspiring, but that's not why we buy. It's why you sell. But we will rarely buy something we don't want, merely because of the passion of the person trying to sell it to us.

Young people today are looking for jobs with deep meaning. I get that. I've raised three of them. We would all love to make an impact in our world. However, not everyone has that luxury. Most businesses don't make a huge impact on the world, but they certainly help you pay your bills, feed your family, and send your kids to college. And while your teens may be eyeing that college degree in philosophy, I don't think a lot of philosophy firms are hiring right now.

As a professional speaker, I see countless aspiring colleagues led astray by well-meaning friends who encourage them to "get out and tell your story." And while I appreciate that you survived cancer and have a story to tell, you need to know that over sixteen million cancer survivors are currently living in the United States alone. Over five thousand people have successfully climbed to the top of Mount Everest, many of them twice. Nearly eighteen thousand former NFL players are still alive today, and two million Americans have lost at least one limb. For meeting planners looking for unique messages and messengers, passion is not enough.

Focusing on your passion is a luxury reserved for the wealthiest among us. The rest of us need to focus on a solid business model of trading value for fair compensation. We need to take passion out of our marketing and have a clear target for who, with money, needs what we are offering. We must have a way to find contacts and turn them into leads, and leads into legitimate prospects and prospects into paying clients. If you are passionate about your business as well, all the better, but it's certainly not required.

Pragmatism trumps idealism. Of course, my three idealistic Millennial offspring will disagree with me on this point, but they have that luxury as two of the three don't have to pay their own bills . . . yet.

Make no mistake, there are some very successful idealists in business, and the successful ones are impacting millions, but only because they have a solid business model that generates real dollars. Your passion will certainly help you get up in the morning, but your business savvy, competitive advantages, and hard work will help you feed your family.

Instead of focusing on your passion, focus on your value proposition, business model, and the needs and wants of your customers. Work your tail off. Be strategic, diligent, persuasive, different, frugal, and demonstrate your value better than others who are competing for your audience. Craft your words, authentically connect with your buyers, and close that sale!

I am passionate about my work on stage as a business speaker and my impact on my consulting clients. But in my marketing, I don't talk about my passion. I talk about their business, their needs, and my unique solutions to their problems. In my business, I focus on building my client list and supporting my employees and my family. I don't spend my work days talking about what is important to me, but what is important to my customers and their business. Of course, if those messages are in alignment, then I will be far more persuasive and happy in my work.

There is no shortage of companies sparked from the passion of their founders. Whether it is a passion for cooking, advocacy, automobiles, or music technology, plenty of these companies have found success—but are by no means the majority. In fact, the vast majority of ventures fail for the simple reason that they were unable to attract enough customers. Their passion gave them a reason to pursue the venture, but they failed on the business or marketing side.

When the company is about you, your passion, and your dreams and ambitions, you have two strikes against you. As a prospective customer, it is not my job to help you live out your life's ambition or follow your dreams. My only role is to purchase something I may want or need. And even then, you have to be a better choice for some legitimate reason. The fact that you dedicated you life to a vegan existence and are committed to providing that alternative for others, means little if your food doesn't taste great and you don't have strong marketing. We come to you to buy, not to be indoctrinated.

I spoke to a gentleman who was interested in some marketing assistance for his company that manufactured portable solar-powered generators. These well-crafted energy devices provided quiet power in remote locations for campers, concerts, trade shows, and street fairs, as well as tiny houses and even so-called "doomsday preppers." Pretty cool solar power generators to be sure.

Unfortunately, visitors to the website were bombarded with his personal crusade to save the planet. Smack dab in the middle of his home page, he featured his mission to reduce greenhouse gas emissions, provide sustainable options to fight global warming, and encourage a shift in our thinking about how we take care of our Mother Earth.

A noble cause to be sure, but what of the countless potential customers who don't share his priorities? It's not that people don't care about the planet, it's that we choose the causes that are important to us, and most, quite frankly, have other priorities including family, school, church, and so on. Put another way: our job is not to help this guy fulfill his mission.

The assumption too often with those who are on a crusade is that if they just explain it enough, they can get others to agree with them and support their cause.

On our first phone call, I asked him if his company was a 501(c)(3) not-for-profit organization. "No," he said, somewhat surprised. "We are an energy company."

"Then why all the preaching about your cause?" I asked.

"Well, that's why I started the company," he responded. "To make an impact."

"But what does that have to do with the trade-show booth I am setting up that I want to power at the state fair?" I ask.

Trying to respect his views, I made it clear that only a fraction of his prospective customers were going to buy because they want to join his crusade to save the Earth. Most prospects are simply looking for a quality power solution that will work well in remote locations, without the noise of a generator or the smell of fumes. Many may even like the optics of supporting responsible power generation, but they are buying for reasons that work for them.

Most of his messaging, or at least the up-front content, was aimed at less than 10 percent of his prospective customers! The other 90 percent don't care about his mission but would love his products. I'm not suggesting that you bury your values, but just don't lead with them if they are irrelevant to your audience.

In the late 1990s, there was a push by education and environmental advocates to build the first-ever aquarium in Denver, Colorado. Being landlocked, Denver is hardly known for its abundant marine life, besides the the world-class rainbow trout in its lakes and mountain streams.

People in the Western and Central states had little exposure to the wonders of the ocean, and supporters felt this could be a great way to bring the ocean to the mountains. Led by a husband and wife team of marine biologists, a consortium of public and private entities came together to build the largest aquarium from Los Angeles to Chicago.

When the doors opened on June 21, 1999, on a prime spot right outside downtown Denver, the crowds were huge and the lines were long. It seems as if they did everything right. The marketing campaign and news media coverage dominated the airwaves. The building was stunning. Massive tanks were filled with an astonishing array of marine life extracted from oceans around the world. Even the fish collection efforts from ocean locations across the globe were well documented, and the footage played on local news. To top it off, live Sumatran tigers found their place in the above-water ecosystem displays.

I was a part of that crowd as we took our kids through the exhibit during the opening week. About fifteen minutes into the journey, I remarked that they would be out of business within two years.

Why? Because it became abundantly clear that the founders' vision of teaching us about ecosystems was being realized. They wanted us to understand how important it was that we protect and conserve the environment. They wanted us to know what we, as humans, are doing to destroy our planet and the marine life within it. What they forgot to ask—or didn't even care ask—was what *we* wanted and were willing to pay for. And while many shared their beliefs, we thought we were buying entertainment; they were on a mission to convert or indoctrinate the masses. We wanted to see cool fish. They want to present a worst-case scenario for the planet if we didn't change our ways. They went bankrupt in April of 2002, less than three years after opening their doors.

At a total cost to build of $93 million, Colorado Ocean Journey was purchased by Landry's Seafood House for $13.6 million. Today, reconfigured for entertainment and known as the Downtown Aquarium (with seafood restaurants inside), it flourishes.

Of course there are examples of mission-driven, crowd-funded ventures that gained attention and generated sales (Bombas socks) because of their message. But they are a fraction of a fraction of a fraction of business success stories. You can point to a billionaire and say, "Well, they never graduated from high school, and they are successful!" It doesn't mean that's the model you should emulate.

WHY YOU DO IT:

We've been conditioned to follow our dreams. We've been told that our customers need to know our "why" before they buy. Uh, no they don't. They need to know *their* why. Why do they need to buy what you are selling? Why are you a better choice than your competitors? Why do they need to make this investment now? Not why you want to live your dreams. We tend to promote what is important to us because it is important to us. The real question is: What is important to your customers?

WHY WE HATE IT:

We don't understand why you're bringing a megaphone to our quiet dinner. We don't appreciate a sermon when we just want a smoothie. They say the sweetest sound to the human ear is the sound of your own name. As customers, we want you to talk about us. It's not that you should bury your dreams. Just don't expect us to share in your dreams. They're *your* dreams. We're not insensitive; we're just indifferent to your cause if it has nothing to do why we are buying from you.

A BETTER APPROACH:

Keep in mind that your customers don't need to believe what you believe in order to buy what you are selling. More importantly, every moment that you spend talking about your passion, you are missing an opportunity to talk about what is important to them.

There is a great exercise where you review all of your own promotional material, anything about you listed on your website, in your brochures, sales sheets, and all the rest. Highlight everything you say about yourself, your qualifications, credentials, mission, passion, etc., with your yellow highlighter. Now, look at the same material and highlight any content you have written about your prospects and customers, their needs, problems, and so on in green.

Take a look and see which color wins out. If there is more yellow than green (and there generally is because we love to talk about ourselves), then you need to revisit your marketing. It's not about you. It's about your customers.

12

My Call Is *Not* Very Important to You

*Time is more valuable than money. You can get
more money, but you cannot get more time.*
–Jim Rohn

The concept of "hell" (stay with me here) has come to mean two very different things in our lexicon: On the positive side, it connotes something that is quite good or impressive.

"That was a hell of a party last night!"

"She is a hell of a good dancer. Dang!"

On the negative side, "hell" is more literal and can allude to something very difficult.

"It was hell trying to loosen that bolt!"

"Bloody hell! I told you that boy was no good!"

The most common imagery comes from the biblical view of hell as a place that you are sentenced to because of some heinous infraction or moral failing. Picture an endless sea of sinners drowning in lava or surrounded by fire and the deafening sounds of their agonizing screams. Overseeing it all is the devil, delighting in the pain. (Or maybe that's just the Hollywood version.)

"She went through hell and back to get out of that marriage."

"Working for him was a living hell!"

With that in mind, it's worth noting that our vernacular commonly connects the words "voicemail" with the word "hell." It's even more notable that the term "voicemail hell" needs no additional explanation or clarification. We've been there. We've lived there, more often than we would like.

And just as it is said that success is not about the destination, but the journey, so too is the road to hell. It's not about having to leave a message for someone you are trying to reach (bad enough); it's about the horrific journey we are forced to travel through your voicemail menu (hell) to even get to the point where we can leave a message. It's a journey we did not ask for. It's a journey we don't want to be on, and we are frustrated with you for making us go there.

The meaning of the phrase "Your call is very important to us" has changed over the years. Thirty years ago, it meant simply, "Your call is very important to us." Today it means "Blah, blah, blah. Go to hell. Blah, blah, blah."

When your recorded hold message tells us over and over "your call is very important us," we hear something different each time you say it.

The first time we hear: "We are talking to another customer. We'll get to you when we are done."

The second time: "I honestly have no idea how long this other person will take. Hang on if you want. We don't really care."

The third time: "It's pretty clear we had budget cuts and we are significantly understaffed. I know you're getting angry and will probably take it out on me. What do you want me to do? I'm underpaid as it is!"

The forth time: "I can't believe you are still holding. Chances are growing by the moment that you will eventually hang up (or we will simply disconnect you) and we won't have to deal with your anger."

The fifth time: "Bite me."

The sixth time: "Pathetic."

The seventh time: "Hang up!"

The eighth time: "Go to hell."

Perhaps this is merely the conversation going on in my head, though many of you will feel the same. This is what I hear you saying as I put everything else in my life on hold hoping you will answer your freaking phone. This is what I hear as my ear begins to get sore and I switch my phone to the other side of my head and tap my foot impatiently. This is what I hear as I have to go to the bathroom and wish I would have called you on my cell phone, so I could just take it in the bathroom with me, but I am not about to leave my office phone and give up after waiting for thirty-eight minutes.

Is this what you're really saying? Does it really matter? It's what we hear that is important. We are your customers, and like you, we don't like waiting on hold forever, or leaving a message. Answer your phone!

In a 2015 study by call analytics firm Invoca, 75 percent of customers were more likely to leave for a competitor after a single negative phone experience. Even worse, 30 percent were more likely to leave a negative online review.[1]

Companies pay lip service to the concept of "valuing the customer." Oh, you value the sale, to be sure. You value the revenue, but do you really value the people behind it? If you did, you would more consistently value their time, their opinions, and their desire to communicate with you on a personal level.

This is not to say that there aren't circumstances that require a brief hold, or a staffer being unavailable. We may be impatient and demanding, but we aren't entirely unreasonable. The challenge for us is when we don't know if we've begun the one time, "your call is very important to us," or the forty-five-minute, twenty-two verses of "your call is very important to us" call. We have no way of knowing at the outset.

Of course, there are other organizations where we have no option. If we want to reach the IRS, we are at their mercy. According to a report from the Taxpayer Advocate Service, featured in Money Magazine, only 37 percent of the calls made to the IRS customer service line leading up to the April 15th tax deadline in 2015 were actually answered.[2] That means 63 percent of the callers got sick of waiting and hung up. The average wait time for those who did manage to get through to customer service was twenty-three minutes, though others could have waited much longer before giving up.

If your customers do have a choice, you need to give them a greater degree of confidence and predictability. A couple of solutions:

Provide an estimated wait time. Give me a realistic expectation of my wait time, so I can adjust my workload accordingly to be ready when you are ready.

You could also include the option to receive a call back at my phone number when a representative is available. This allows me to go about my day and not lose thirty-five minutes waiting for what will ultimately be a two-minute call.

Even if you don't believe this issue applies to you and your business, there is no question that it resonates with you. We have all been on the receiving end of this abuse. This service deficiency is never so apparent as when you are looking to resolve a problem or issue with a vendor or service provider. There is a universal disdain for company phone-tree systems, yet their use (and abuse) is pervasive.

Staff appropriately. And appropriateness is dictated by the needs of your customers, not merely your cash flow. If you can't afford enough staff to serve your customers, then something is seriously wrong with your business model. Your pricing, hours of operation, expense management, and product offering should combine to create a profitable structure that serves your owners, staff, and customers. If you're out of balance (a constant struggle for most), then the "odd man out" should not be your customers. Those who bring in revenue (your customers), and their perception of you, should be paramount in your mind and strategic planning.

The amount of revenue you are losing from the customers you're angering and repelling should be sufficient in many cases to hire more staff to cover your phones. Your bean counters can show you the cost savings of understaffing your customer service line, call-center team, or even firing your receptionist, but what you are missing is the lost revenue from those whom you have frustrated, angered, or inconvenienced. When you undervalue our time and overestimate our patience, we leave you for competitors as soon as another option becomes available.

WHY YOU DO IT:

You purchase and implement horrible phone systems because you believe that you are striking a balance between efficiency and availability. In most cases, you aren't. You feel good during your workday because your team is receiving far fewer calls and you are freed up to do what you think you should be doing. Those pesky customers are out of sight and out of mind. *"We are a well-oiled machine!"* you think to yourself because you don't hear many complaints. I would submit that you aren't hearing complaints very often because those who would complain are buying from your competitors!

WHY WE HATE IT:

How do I hate thee? Let me count the ways. We hate to be on hold. We hate not knowing how long we are going to be on hold. We hate how we behave when a rep finally answers the phone. We hate the time we lose, and we hate having to navigate your horrible phone system when a real person could have directed us to the proper extension quickly. Finally, we hate to listen closely as your menu options have changed. And the truth is: you hate it too!

A BETTER APPROACH:

Do you know who is really good at directing phone calls to the right person or department? People. Real-life, breathing, thinking, speaking people. The good news is that you probably know a few. Just sayin'.

13

Don't Treat Me Like You Want to Be Treated

*To understand the man, you must first
walk a mile in his moccasins.
–Native American saying (adapted from
a poem by Mary T. Lathrap)*

The primary reason why most people in business don't know how to deliver a great customer experience is they've rarely experienced it for themselves. We generally engage in reasonable transactions and we sporadically deliver good service. But the experiences that are worth repeating and worth sharing are few and far between because we train merely for the transaction and the strong service delivery. To actually delight and connect with a customer requires a deeper understanding of them, and few companies know how to do that well.

"You don't understand," the exasperated woman said to the customer service rep. "I have tried everything to get this Wi-Fi thing working, and I can't get coverage in my own house!"

"Are you near the unit?" Randy the tech-support rep asked. (You know what's coming next.) "I need to you to unplug the base unit, wait thirty seconds, and plug it back in."

"You are the third person I have talked to, and everyone tells me the same damn thing!" she exploded at the rep. "Of course I have unplugged it and plugged it back in. I need to get this fixed! I'm sorry, but I'm very frustrated!"

"Okay, I understand," Randy continued. "So, you've tried unplugging it. Hmm. How many devices are connected to the Wi-Fi?"

"None! Zero! Nobody is connected! That's why I am calling you!"

We can all empathize with this woman, right? The rep didn't do anything wrong and is feeling the brunt of her frustration. The woman didn't do anything wrong. She's paying for service that she can't seem to connect to. Both sides are justified in what they feel and say. What is missing in this interaction?

What's missing is "service empathy"—a real understanding of the woman (a frazzled working mom of three kids) and the deeper root of her exasperation. From the rep's perspective (single guy, goes to community college, works nights for the cable company), the woman is irrational and needs to calm down so they can go through the protocol to fix the problem.

What the support rep doesn't know is that this single mom worked all day, picked up her son from daycare, got home an hour ago, and still hasn't even taken off her jacket. Her sixteen-year-old daughter is freaking out because she has a term paper due in her sophomore history class and can't get online. Her six-year-old daughter just broke her new iPad after hitting it a dozen times trying to get the game to load, and her three-year-old son has been in daycare all day and just wants some attention—and she hasn't even started making dinner!

While the problem still has to be resolved, the level of service empathy can be greatly enhanced with a better understanding of the people on the other end of that phone, their lives, their days, and their needs. It's more than getting the Wi-Fi to work, it's the catalyst for everything that can—and is—going wrong for this amazing mom tonight.

But how could Randy the rep possibly know all of this? Well, he could have had a good idea, if he would have been trained properly, and not just on technical aspects of his job, but on the behavioral, social, emotionally intelligent aspects of the job. It's a matter of training and culture within the company—if they care enough to make this a priority. These issue are knowable. This heightened level of understanding and empathy from active listening and problem-solving could take the company far when it comes to customer retention—the lifeblood of business.

Here is a revised scenario bolstered by a heightened level of service empathy:

"Ms. Gelman, I know how frustrating this can be," the service rep said with true understanding in his voice. "I promise you, we will get this resolved, and I will not leave you until it is fixed and working for everyone in your house. Okay?"

"Okay. Thank you!"

"Is that your child crying in the background? Do you need to tend to him? I am happy to wait on the line if you need to go help him. Take your time. Don't worry. I am not going anywhere."

Both scenarios are likely to resolve the problem, but which approach fosters loyalty, connection, and a legitimate feeling of being served? Which one is going to diminish the likelihood that this busy mom will complain to her friends or her online connections about how much she hates her cable company? Did the second scenario cost the company more money? Of course not. And it will likely result in increased revenue from bolstered loyalty.

This is more than merely being understanding and providing service. For many businesses, this is a matter of survival. Especially when it comes to frustrated customers, how you resolve problems can make or break your company.

My father used to caution us to be mindful in gift-giving. He would say that most people buy gifts for others that they would like to receive themselves, rather than what the other would want. That, of course, is true in romantic relationships as well. Pity the hapless husband who buys his wife a tool or electronic gadget that *he* wants for *her* birthday or Mother's Day. Smart people buy their loved ones what they know *they* would want. It is the same in business. Give them the service that they want—not the way that you would want it.

We are often taught in life to follow the Golden Rule and "Do unto others as you would have them do unto you." But in business, we can't assume that our customers want what we want. To the contrary, most of our customers are not us. Not even close. Their lives are different, their needs are different, and their priorities are different. It's only when we can truly walk in their shoes that we can adopt the right mindset, and create a customer experience journey to serve them as they wish to be served.

So, when we ask our employees to treat our customers as we would want to be treated, there is often a disconnect. Your sixteen-year-old cashier might want to be treated in a way that demands very little of him. He may love the ideas of others finding him attractive or praising him for his sense of humor. He may love to banter with coworkers or customers. He may hate to feel rushed, or love to talk about his new car or count how may people liked his Instagram post. He is sixteen years old, for crying out loud!

Then again, your customer might be a forty-five-year-old business consultant. She's been traveling all day after being delayed on her last of three flights and stopped in on the way home from the airport because she needs to grab food for her kids who got home four hours ago from school and have been texting her about being "starving" ever since. She's dealing with exhaustion, mommy guilt, work pressure, and digestive issues. She wants to get her order and just get out of there.

Of course, your frontline employees just see a disheveled, impatient woman in a wrinkly business suit who clearly is not interested in chitchat. Do you want your people to treat her like they want to be treated or to understand how she wants to be treated? If it were up to her, she would prefer to be treated with understanding and empathy, respect and kindness. Mostly, she wants speed and efficiency.

If you train your people to understand the various profiles of your customers, they can tailor their approach and add it to their foundational behaviors of kindness, efficiency, cheerfulness, and the rest.

As of this writing, Chik-fil-A is poised to overtake Burger King, Wendy's, and Taco Bell, becoming the third largest fast-food retailer in the United States—behind McDonald's and Starbucks. The fact that they are closed on Sundays makes their rise and success that much more remarkable. And while the chicken is good, it's the legendary service that makes them stand out from the pack. They hire for it, train for it, and reinforce it constantly.

According to a *QSR* magazine's annual "Drive-Thru Study" released in 2016:

Employees at Chick-fil-A were the most likely of the 15 chains surveyed to say "please" and "thank you," and to smile at drive-thru customers. Chick-fil-A workers were also the second most likely to have a "pleasant demeanor," only topped by the up-and-coming fast-food chain PDQ.

You may wonder if this is really that complicated. I mean, respect is respect, right? Good service is good service, and a smile is a smile. We all know what that is. Well, yes and no. We certainly understand and can agree on what attention, courtesy, and manners look like. It's when things are busy, customers are stressed out, and we are challenged that this level of service empathy really bears fruit.

It's recognizing that the mother with an infant and two other kids might need assistance bringing the meal to their table. It's understanding the reason that the airline passenger is upset that his seat (that he booked three months ago) was changed as he embarks with a loved one on a twenty-three-hour flight. It's the working mom with a one-hour window to get her dry cleaning picked up before she heads to a parent-teacher conference.

What happens in your brief interaction is filtered through more than the stress of your day, it's the reality of theirs. Sure, both are important, but your level of empathy and accommodation is a direct reflection of your understanding—truly understanding your customers. This is more than good business; it's a good life lesson and can become a legitimate competitive advantage.

To walk a mile in someone's moccasins requires a legitimate effort to map out who your customers are and understanding their days, their pressures, and what is on their plate. If you service a specific industry or demographic, create a sketch of the people who make up that group.

Creating a culture of service requires more than your intention and the verbal reinforcement of that mantra. You have to take steps to understand your customers better and treat them, not like you would want to be treated, but like they would.

WHY YOU DO IT:

Conventional wisdom dictates that we all want to be treated well, with courtesy and kindness. We say to our team: "This is our core value folks! Treat your customers as you would want to be treated. The customer is king. Treat them that way!" Of course, how that is filtered, understood, and delivered can vary wildly. If you can't truly define it, how can you measure it and evaluate its delivery?

WHY WE HATE IT:

A pervasive challenge in business is the across-the-board inconsistency in the delivery of service. We never know what we're going to get, and so we (your customers) have stopped expecting good service. Even when done well, our description of great service is simply speed, kindness, and responsiveness. We don't expect empathy, accommodation, anticipation, and enthusiasm.

A BETTER APPROACH:

Forget the rule of thumb in regard to treating customers. As they say, rules of thumb are only good for counting thumbs. Consider a day in the life of your customers (DLOC). Bolster your training to include service empathy. Research it, describe it, discuss it. Role-play scenarios with your team and have them change roles. Give them note cards describing who they are with details about their life, job, challenges, and other facts. See if others can guess, by the interaction, details of their life.

The idea is that your team should rarely have to figure out or navigate a situation for the first time. If they experience it a few times in their training, they will be well-prepared on your front lines. With this foundation, you'll create a greater connection with your customers, and your team will be prepared to deal with them the way *they* want to be treated.

14

DON'T PASS THE BUCK (AND DON'T THROW COWORKERS UNDER THE BUS)

The moment you are old enough to take the
wheel, responsibility lies with you.
–J. K. Rowling

There is an oft-told story of a company CEO who sat in the lobby of his own building and watched as employee after employee passed a crumpled piece of paper on the floor. Eventually, a member of the housekeeping staff swept it up on his regular rounds as he passed by. At a later staff meeting, the CEO told his team of his experience and asked whose job it is to pick up the trash in the lobby. Of course, the answer is: everyone's.

Passing the buck in an organization can take two forms: passive and active. Both can have a devastating effect on your business.

Passive abdication of responsibility can manifest by ignoring a problem (like something needing cleaning), a ringing phone, or a customer clearly looking for assistance. The "It's not my job" or "They don't pay me for that" mentality can have an insidious effect on an organization.

My friend the late, great Brad Hams wrote books and spoke about a concept he called "ownership thinking." He spent his last years helping organizations create an internal employee mindset to treat their jobs, not merely as jobs, but as if they had ownership—both literally and figuratively. How would your people act differently if they felt they had a stake in the success of your business?

With an ownership mindset, your people no longer passively ignore obvious problems or pressing issues because they are always looking for ways to be of service and build the business, not just do their jobs.

The active "buck passers" deliberately push problems or blame to others. It's a lot easier to transfer a call to someone else than to take the initiative to help the customers get what they need. Of course, in many instances, others are better equipped to handle a situation, but even in these cases, customers will become very frustrated if they have to spend twenty minutes trying to resolve a problem, only to be passed on to someone else and have to start over. We've all been there.

In the worst scenarios, staffers throw their coworkers or others under the bus in front of, or in conversations with customers. This is worse than mere gossip in front of customers (bad enough). It's actively shifting blame to others to save your reputation and demeaning the organization in the process.

"Sorry. Shipping screws this up constantly!" the exasperated sales rep complained to the prospect inquiring about a late delivery. And while the sales rep gets off the hook in his mind, the company's reputation has suffered and the customer relationship is at risk.

These aren't isolated instances. The temptation to shift blame to avoid the uncomfortable interaction or refusing to take blame for something that is truly not your fault is pervasive. The problem is that the customer doesn't really care who is at fault. Their ego isn't threatened. They just want the problem solved! It's not an individual's behavior, it's a cultural issue. It's a management training issue. The behavior needs to be pointed out and addressed on a company-wide basis, with discussion about scenarios, role-playing, and more.

Lest you think I am immune, I too have found myself succumbing to this easy-out behavior. This is an excerpt from a mea culpa that I wrote that made its way around the world many years ago when I was leading CEO groups for Vistage International:

I just got my lunch handed to me by a business prospect and will be eating humble pie for months to come. It was a humiliating lesson, exacted upon a careless and overly casual professional by an astute and thoughtful company leader. File this under "Do as I say, not as I do."

I arrived this afternoon for my third face-to-face meeting with a strong prospect for the Vistage CEO roundtable group that I lead in Denver. I'll call him Mike. Assuming this was the final step of the evaluation process with an impressive company leader, I believed that Mike and I both had found a strong fit and would likely be progressing with a formal membership application. He would join my CEO roundtable group, and I would be his executive coach.

After moving beyond the greetings and pleasantries, we took our seats in his office as Mike closed the door. As he sat by his desk, he began our discussion by explaining that he had been struggling that week with an internal dynamic at his company whereby his customer service staff and administration staff were bad-mouthing each other. Worse yet, they were expressing dissatisfaction with their coworker in conversations with customers of the company. He explained that when a customer called with a complaint about their bill or the service that had been provided, a staffer from admin would say that the customer service department had clearly dropped the ball, or customer service would throw admin under the bus by blaming them for whatever the problem was. He was struggling with how best to confront the situation.

Mike continued: "Then I got this voicemail message last Friday," and he turned to the phone on his desk, hit the speakerphone button, and began to dial. To my surprise, the voice on the recording was my own.

"Hi Mike," I said. "This is David Avrin, and yes, you are correct, the meeting place listed in the email invitation was wrong. Some bonehead from the corporate office sent out the wrong location." Then, without ever taking his gaze off of me, Mike pressed a button on the phone rewinding it slightly. "Some bonehead from the corporate office . . ." Click. "Some bonehead from the corporate office . . ." Click. "Some bonehead from the corporate office . . ." Click. "Some bonehead from the corporate office . . ."

I sat speechless as Mike leaned back in his chair, and after a brief pause, looked me in the eye and said, "So here's my dilemma, Dave. I'm looking for an executive coach to help me become a better leader and deal with issues such as how to confront poor internal behavior, and this message is what I received from my leading candidate. What do I do with this?"

As he spoke, all I could do was nod knowingly, acknowledging that everything he was saying was true and the concern he expressed was richly deserved. I had screwed up—big time. Not just because my poorly considered, offhand comment had violated my covenant with a trusted and valued corporate partner, but because I had damaged my credibility with someone I respected and was hoping to earn his respect. It was careless, and the resulting challenge to my judgment and credibility was no one's fault but my own.

In that moment, wanting to go throw up, I knew the worst thing I could do was to attempt an excuse or try to talk *around the massive elephant clearly sitting in the middle of the room. Instead, I acknowledged what we both knew to be true. I screwed up. I offered my apology and told him that he was right to call me out on my poor behavior and that I knew it had damaged my credibility.*

I explained that in my effort to be overly casual in my correspondence and maybe even a little bit "cool," I used a very poor choice of words. More likely, by casually dismissing or even denigrating someone else (for what was clearly an honest mistake), I was basically implying that I would never be guilty of such an infraction. Of course, we all make mistakes, and ascribing blame, regardless of the legitimacy, was clearly wrong.

As I flashed back to my frustrated state when I made the phone call to Mike following the errant email blast, I realized that my remarks were simply a poorly considered, knee-jerk reaction (emphasis on "jerk") to a situation that I feared would damage his perception of me and our organization. Instead, my actions diminished our credibility. So, once again, all I could do was apologize.

We went on to have a solid and meaningful discussion about the value of our leadership roundtable and his prospective involvement, but the reality of what had transpired hung over the conversation. It was clear that my professional reputation with this company leader was tarnished—by my behavior. It was a bell that couldn't be unrung. He ultimately did join a CEO roundtable group—just not mine.

That day, I stunk up the place. The next day, I did better. Mea culpa.

When your employees focus on ascribing responsibility (blame) rather than taking responsibility, the reputation of the company suffers, the customer relationship suffers, and clients are lost.

One of the most atrocious and high-profile cases involved the now-defunct telecommunications provider Qwest (now CenturyLink, to some extent). Federal regulators discovered that the company's customer service department was, in fact, their sales department. When customers called with complaints, they were transferred to a sales rep who feigned solving their problem. Of course, the solution was to upgrade their service to something that worked better for the company. The bigger problem was that when the reps realized that upset customers weren't going to buy anything, they told them they were forwarding them to a manager to solve the problem, but were actually just sending them back to the queue to talk to another sales rep. The dissatisfied customers were now someone else's problem.

From your customer's perspective, passing the buck creates two massive problems: One, it delays the resolution of the issue. The customer's frustration increases with every passing minute and every handoff to another employee and another on hold or, worse yet, voicemail. Second, it demonstrate to your clients that you are not a well-oiled machine. It's bad enough that something didn't go right, but now they wonder if the problem will get fixed at all, when and by whom.

WHY YOU DO IT:

Deflecting problems is a "skill" most of us learned at an early age. Whether it was to avoid responsibility or avoid the work needed to address the situation, passing the buck meant passing off the problem. Neither one demonstrates the best human characteristic.

WHY WE HATE IT:

We need someone to step up and be a hero. It's going to get addressed eventually, so why delay or deflect? We need someone to take ownership and stop wasting our time by passing the buck.

A BETTER APPROACH:

Teach your people to own your customers' problems, and let them be the heroes for solving them. People will pass off problems if there is a culture that allows or supports it. Don't feed that culture. Change the culture to one of accountability and problem-solving. Reward it, incentivize it, hold people accountable, and celebrate small victories.

15

STOP MAKING US DO YOUR WORK

Nothing is really work unless you would
rather be doing something else.
–J. M. Barrie

Whether it is in the interest of expediency, efficiency, or simply because you don't want to pay anyone to do it yourself, the number of responsibilities being pushed to your customers is growing to an absurd level.

After shopping for our own groceries today, we go through self-checkout, scan at the machine, pay the machine, bag them ourselves, and then we take them to our car. With the exception of the shopping itself, every one of those tasks used to be performed by an employee.

Think about all the things that used to be done for us. It's not that people were lazy; businesses just worked harder to compete for our business—and service was a recognizable and expected deliverable. The customer was king or queen, and we were treated as such. There is a famous scene in the movie *Back to the Future* where Marty McFly goes into his town square in the 1950s and marvels at how different things were in the past.

One of the funnier moments in the movie was when a car pulled into the 1950s gas station and was "attacked" by four station attendants who immediately began washing the car's windshield, pumping the gas, filling the tires, and checking the oil. All of this while the family sat comfortably in their car. My kids looked at me with bewilderment, but us Baby Boomers laughed and sighed at what used to be. It wasn't a NASCAR pit stop. It was life in the 1950s and 1960s.

In the 1970s, the advent of self-serve gasoline was actually offered as a cost savings. Full-service was still the norm, but self-serve was a couple of cents per gallon cheaper. Of course today, there is one option that isn't really an option: If you want gas, get out in the snow or rain and pump it.

Is it really a big deal to have to pump your own gas? Not really. But it is indicative of so many tasks that have been shifted to the customers. Some make sense and are appreciated—primarily those that allow us to complete tasks from our cell phone or from the privacy of our own home. But it's the point-of-purchase, customer-facing tasks that begin to grate on us, and once again, that is not the feeling you want your customers to have when dealing with you.

Service reduction in many cases is a direct reflection of not hiring staff to perform the functions we had become

accustomed to. While much of the "make them do it themselves" mentality is clearly a function of cost-cutting, other
cases are misguided automation strategies driven by technology and those that sell it.

Making your patients fill in their own information on
the doctor's office intake form on their Internet-connected
tablets is a solution looking for a problem. Checking things
off on a clipboard with a pencil was fast and easy. Navigating your technology is a pain. Of course, it will become easier once we get the hang of it, but we don't do it every day
(like they do). We are there just that day. In fact, if we are
in the doctor's office, we likely feel like crap, or have an injured child needing to be seen. The technology salesperson
sold you a bill of goods that it was going to save you time
and make you more efficient. Uh . . . by making your sick or
injured patient do it for you . . . *before* they can be seen by a
doctor? Why do we have to navigate your technology? That's
your job! We just want to be treated for our ailments.

Of course, not all do-it-yourself tasks are unappreciated.
We love to be able to transfer money between accounts on
our cell phone without having to go to the bank, but we don't
like having to bag our own groceries. We love to avoid driving to court and simply pay our parking fine online, but we
hate having to tag our own luggage at the airport. In fact, I
simply roll my bags to the agent and say, "Hi. You're better
at this this. I would appreciate it if you would do it instead."
Then they might say, "Here. Let me show you how to do it." I
just politely decline.

You may think I am being elitist, but I assure you, I am
not. I'm just busy, and I expect professionals to do their part.
If they will do theirs, then I will do mine. By the way, my

part is to give them my business and my money. If they fail to do their part effectively and to my liking, then I will take my business elsewhere. This is how a free-market economy works. I will buy from you as long as I am satisfied. When I am no longer satisfied, I will buy from someone else.

When my son was born, the doctor offered me the scissors and asked if I'd like to cut the cord. I politely declined and said with a smile, "Uh, I think you are way more qualified than I am!" I know. Right? (Then again, I had already experienced this "beautiful" Dad moment with the birth of my daughter, Sydney. The magic of the "cord-cutting" moment was gone when my son arrived.)

And while most pushed-to-the-customer responsibilities are admittedly small inconveniences, they do add up over time, take time out of our day, and certainly don't foster greater loyalty. Efficiency and cost-savings for them—additional inconveniences and work for us. Not sure this is stacked in our favor.

I was at the airline check-in counter recently and pointed out to the counter rep that my TSA precheck number was not added to my boarding pass by the gate agent when she printed it during my changed connection. The rep said to me, "Oh, you'll need to call member services to get that fixed." As I was at the counter, I asked if he could fix it on his screen, but he just said that his screen couldn't do it and repeated that I would need to call the airline's other department, and then he turned away from me and began to work with the next person in line.

I thought to myself, "No! I want you to call and fix it. You guys screwed it up. We've been traveling for eighteen hours starting in Bangkok and just arrived from Frankfurt,

Germany. Take some initiative and support your paying client! Why do I have to fix the problem your employee caused? You know your internal systems way better than I do. What you could solve in five minutes will likely take me forty-five minutes, and we have another plane to catch."

But I didn't say it. I wished I had, but I knew that was their company policy. They don't solve problems there at that counter because they have been told not to. Fail.

This is a matter of policy, training, and culture. Don't simply tell us that you value your customers, show us by empowering/requiring your staff to own problems and fix them. Can you just imagine the boost to customer satisfaction? Can you just envision the different scenarios that people might post on their social media pages? One is anger and frustration directed at you, and the other is an exasperating ordeal where you get to be the hero. And both of those shared scenarios will be available to be seen by all until the end of time. Which would you rather have posted?

We talked earlier about being sent to voicemail hell. It's just south of Hades, and no one goes there willingly. Then why do so many send us there when our only offense was having the audacity to want to do business with you? No life of crime. No cruelty to animals. No scams perpetrated on nuns and orphans. Just the gall to call you and hopefully talk to a real person. That call, if answered by a real, knowledgeable person, could send us to the correct staffer or department in mere seconds. Instead, the job of navigating your complex organizational structure has been shifted to us because the cost savings of eliminating these gatekeepers was too alluring to resist.

The customer service question that we wanted to ask, that should have been answered quickly, instead requires hold times often approaching an hour because you failed to take human reactions into account when you decided to hire your customers as your new receptionist—*without pay*.

It's clear that you don't want to answer our questions. You want us to find the answers to our own questions, and we get directed to a Frequently Asked Questions section on your website. You make us scan and search and figure it out for ourselves, when you could have very easily answered it for us. Oh, but you are so tired of answering questions . . . from your customers . . . about your business. I totally get it.

Once again, when we are asked to take on more of the burden in the client/customer relationship, the perceived value for the dollars spent decreases. "Why am I paying a full 20 percent tip to my server, when I served myself from the buffet?" we ask ourselves. "Why should I pay a 6 percent commission to a realtor when the buyer found me on my social media page?"

The goodwill and positive feelings necessary to forge and retain beneficial customer relationships is lost every time another service item is shifted to your customers. When you work so hard to build a business, create products, refine services, and deliver excellence, only to burden those you so desperately want to impress, it is on you.

WHY YOU DO IT:

The primary reason that you shift activities and responsibilities to your customers is to lower your staffing costs and remain price competitive. By and large, expense reduction is a wise move and a smart ongoing strategy. What's the big deal? All your competitors are doing it. It seems basic. People can easily tag their luggage or bag their own groceries. They won't mind. It's not like we are asking much of them.

But it does add up. It adds frustration and resentment and causes some to search for an alternative.

WHY WE HATE IT:

It's just one more inconvenience, especially if we are in a hurry. We think, "You work in this business every day. You have the experience. Why are we having to do your job? I have a job. How about I do my job, and you do your job?"

Worse still, it's not the employees' fault. The company decided to move the task to their paying customer, but the staff person takes the brunt of the frustration and has to put the customer through training to learn the tasks. Dumb.

A BETTER APPROACH:

Always look for efficiency in your business, but if reducing tasks for your employees requires transferring them to your customers, who have a choice of where to buy, then this is a bad idea and likely costing you more than you are saving!

Resist the urge to follow the pack. Call them trends, shifts, or even disruption if you will, but that doesn't make them good or right. Hold off as long as you can, or buck the trend and reintroduce what others have eliminated. It could become a competitive advantage.

If there is a needed service task, then do it for you customers—and do it cheerfully! Your customers will recognize it, appreciate it, and reward you for it with their business and their loyalty.

16

YOUR STALKING IS
CREEPING US OUT

How can I miss you if you won't go away?
–Dan Hicks

Have you ever met somebody who seemed really nice at first? You seemed to have a lot in common, he or she was really fun, and you were drawn to each other in a way? You enjoyed seeing that person and looked forward to connecting. But over time, maybe even rather quickly, your new friend became very needy and started calling or texting you a little too often.

"Hey! What's up? What are you doing? You busy today? Who are you with? What are you doing? Why aren't you texting me back? Are you mad at me? Are you sleeping? What are you doing?"

And you find yourself a bit overwhelmed and trying to find excuses to avoid that person—but he or she just won't stop, and just keeps contacting you over and over and over? When you have autoresponders, send email blasts, or over-survey your customers, you are that person.

Baby Boomers, and most Gen Xers, fondly remember the Sears Wish Book. This amazing holiday catalogue was sent to millions of American homes every fall featuring a vast array of items that were available in Sears physical stores, but could also be ordered and delivered in time for Christmas or Hanukkah. As Sears's heyday was well before the Internet, the Wish Book was as close as we got to Amazon.

My brothers and sister and I would devour the catalogue every fall, dog-ear the pages, and circle things we wanted with a marker. We each got our own pen color and hoped Santa would bring our selections. Our parents shopped for us. We shopped for our siblings. We were so excited to receive this catalogue in the mail each year.

Now, imagine if we got a copy of this catalogue every month—or even every week. What about multiple times a week? It certainly wouldn't be special. It might even become an easy throwaway. Of course, there is a balance between a once-a-year pitch and a daily onslaught. That's what this section is about—balance.

So, we bought from you once. It doesn't mean we want to hear from you every day with a new pitch to buy. Okay, so your numbers might suggest that this tactic works because some people will buy, but I'm not sure you recognize how extraordinarily high the cost has been.

Consider this: Everyone that you have added to your list from your online shopping cart or your in-store purchase is a prequalified buyer—a very good thing! They have already demonstrated that they like you enough to spend their money with you in exchange for the goods and services they want. There is no better prospect than those who have already bought from us.

Now, logic would dictate that these are the customers you want to nurture, treat kindly, and cater to. Of the famed eighty/twenty rule, these are the twenty. Many are even the coveted ten! So, what do you do instead? You bombard them with sales pitches—weekly, daily, or even multiple times a day! The people you should love, you instead annoy. The ones you should treat with kid gloves, you pummel.

Your revenue numbers might suggest a successful tactic. You are making sales to be sure. but the reality is that you have annoyed the majority of your best customers. These are not even prospects, but actual paying customers who have bought from you before! Many, if not most might have continued buying from you for years to come if you had not frustrated them. You are satisfied with continuing sales from a fraction, when you could have had sales from many more for months and years to come.

Instead, you sacrificed them in favor of instant gratification. You could have been great friends, but instead have become that annoying friend we want to avoid. Or worse yet, you are no longer a friend and we can't get you to go away, so we unsubscribe and you've lost us forever. And it could have been such a beautiful relationship, but you blew it by being needy. Dang it!

Another form of unwanted contact is the barrage after social media connection. Put simply, the fact that we connect with you on a social media platform is not an open invitation to immediately launch into a prolonged sales pitch.

"Hmmm, his business looks interesting, I think I'll send a connection request," you think to yourself. Twenty-two seconds later, a four-page autoresponder message begins: "Thanks for connecting. I have a simple question for you. When was the last time you reviewed your financial investment portfolio and asked hard questions about your long-term security?"

Yuck! It's so slimy. I don't know you. You haven't earned the right to launch into a sales pitch. Now is not the time to try to get my money. It makes me regret having ever clicked on your name or invited you to connect at all.

An invitation to connect is merely that—an invitation to connect. It is not permission to try to sell me anything. Worse yet, you know nothing about me, and your verbiage is a clear indication of that.

You want to show me how to write and publish my very own book? Really? I've written five. You want to show me how to get paid to speak? I've been a professional speaker for twenty years. You want to show me how Internet marketing can boost my revenue? I've taught marketing for twenty years. You know nothing about me. Your mail-merge function may put my name at the top of the email, but that level of personalization doesn't cut it, pal. You suck at this!

Can you imagine showing up for a sales meeting having done zero research on the person or company that you are selling to? That's what autoresponders and form letters are. They don't work. Worse yet, they are insulting and offensive. The more often you spam us, the less likely we are to buy.

When we check out of a retail store, we are often asked for our email address. I politely decline. When a young woman rings up my purchase at the register and then asks for my phone number, I tell her that I am flattered, but I'm much too old for her. She will invariably stammer, "No. What I meant was . . ." (Of course, my teens are mortified when I respond this way, which makes it that much more fun to say.)

We are reluctant to give our email address to the person at the register because we know what is coming. We are about to be inundated with an onslaught of marketing pitches and sales specials, in addition to the surveys about our experience. Then our information is sold to others, and they will hound us as well. I just wanted to buy a windshield scraper for my car. I don't want to get married to you or all of your friends.

Once again, these are your best customers and clients! They liked you enough to buy something from you. So these are the people you choose to inundate, annoy, offend, stalk, and overly survey? Oh, you may catch a few in your net, but the vast majority of your best prospects have left you in search of a little peace and quiet. Not exactly spreading goodwill.

Okay, while we're on the subject, just know that relentless surveying turns happy customers into unhappy ones.

We understand that you want to nip potential service delivery problems in the bud. If there is a point of dissatisfaction, you want to find out quickly so that you can correct the problem. More importantly, you want to placate the dissatisfied customer, make them feel heard so they don't go on an online rant or post negative reviews.

Some restaurants have a sign on the wall or even on the tables that reads: "If something is not right, please don't tell

Yelp. Tell us. We'll make it right." Embassy Suites places a small plastic sign on the bathroom counter that essentially says the same thing. The reasons are clear. It's not merely about providing great service, it's the recognition that the ramifications of underperformance are profound. All of that is smart business.

The challenge comes when you seek to extract our opinions—relentlessly. You survey and ask and text and email your guests over and over. Heaven forbid we fail to take ten minutes to evaluate our forty-five-second interaction with you! Not to worry, you will ask again in a day or two. And if by chance we ignore that request, you'll be back stalking us again sooner than later.

Computer-generated emails are like your neighbor's annoying dog sticking his nose in private places; he can seem incredibly friendly, but he lacks the social awareness to realize that he's making you very uncomfortable.

I also recognize that you will inevitably receive less-than-flattering comments online. Not everyone will love you and what you do. That's simply human nature. Generating positive comments on review sites like Yelp, TripAdvisor, Rotten Tomatoes, Glassdoor, and your own website is a smart strategy. But when you ask for a review, comments, or feedback and don't get an immediate response, we are telling you something: We don't want to fill out your form! When you then ask us over and over, day after day, we get frustrated.

The irony of asking for positive reviews from your happy customers—repeatedly—is that you have magically (or tragically) transformed our previously good experience into a bad one. We really liked you, and now we don't because you won't leave us alone.

WHY YOU DO IT:

When it comes to pitching your previous customers, the well-worn maxim holds true: The people most likely to buy from you are the people who have bought previously. It's just smart business to spend time, effort, and dollars marketing to your base. It works in politics and it works in business. Better still, the more data you have on your customers, detailing their buying preferences, the more you can adjust what, how, and when you pitch. Smart strategy. The problem comes from the frequency and lack of personalization.

WHY WE HATE IT:

Quite simply, we are overwhelmed with companies pitching us, stalking us, and pestering us. It may seem reasonable for my son's teacher to give him a big report to write, but when he get overwhelmed by assignments from multiple teachers at the same time, he is frustrated and overwhelmed.

There are companies that I really like. It doesn't mean that I want to hear from them multiple times a week or month. Heck, there are bands that I love to go see. I can't imagine enjoying seeing them every week. And just because I liked one song from that band doesn't mean I want to be constantly pitched every song they've ever recorded or will record.

A BETTER APPROACH:

Space it out. You want your customers to look forward to hearing from you. Play the long game. You are correct that marketing to your previous customers is a smart strategy, but over-marketing to anyone, let alone your best customers, is a terrible strategy. Stop it!

As for surveying, ask once—maybe even twice, but no more and never again. You know darned well that computer programs exist that can limit the number of times a message will go out. You are shooting yourself in the foot if you survey every customer after every transaction or interaction and repeat your request ad nauseam.

17

Avoid the Sin of Omission

Excellence is the unlimited ability to improve
the quality of what you have to offer.
–Rick Pitino

"Hey! Why does she get two chicken fingers and I only get one?" the four-year-old at the next table whined. "That's not fair!"

"You got one big piece, and she got two little ones," their mom responded, trying to keep the peace. "It's all the same!"

But to a four-year-old, it isn't the same. He looked past what he did have and was fixated on what he didn't. It's human nature. Whether you call it the glass being half empty or struggling to focus on the positive, what they don't have will always dominate the minds of most. Too often in business, it's what we don't have or don't offer that can make or break our experience and leave our customers less than satisfied.

Do you offer Wi-Fi, gluten-free or vegan options, weekend hours, childcare, or a baby-changing station? Do you have a nonsmoking section, wheelchair accessibility, menus with larger type, or electrical outlets to charge our cell phones while we shop or dine? In this rapidly changing world of technology, creative amenities, and a seemingly out-of-control gluten-free movement, you will sometimes drive us away by what you *don't* offer.

I have stood in line to be seated at an airport restaurant watching person after person ask the hostess if there are any tables with an electrical outlet nearby, only to be told, "We don't have any tables with outlets." Then those prospects leave, one by one, another and another. Lost business. Lost revenue because there are no power outlets? Is this not an easy fix? Wouldn't the profit from three or four customers cover the costs of the new outlets? What are your customers wanting and expecting that you don't provide? Trust me. You are losing customers to competitors.

Do you have a system in place to track requests from customers? Is it merely anecdotal and occasionally and informally passed on to leadership, or documented by those in charge and acted upon? How many people have asked for a specific menu item or alteration (gluten-free options, a vegetarian choice)? Are people asking about Wi-Fi, power outlets, smoking areas, kid friendly, or kid free?

Why isn't there a phone number on your website? Oh, yeah. You don't want your customers to call you. Dumb.

Why don't you offer Wi-Fi? Oh, yeah. You don't want your customers to stay too long. Not to worry. Many of them won't come at all, or they won't come back. Problem solved.

There was a scene in the Tom Hanks movie *The Wonders* (one of my favorites!) where the father of the main character is reading the newspaper at work and shaking his head. As the owner of an appliance store, he is lamenting that a new competitor is now open on Sundays. "I don't think I want to live in a country where you have to open on Sundays," he sighs.

Of course, today everything is available at every hour of the day and night. The only businesses that aren't are local retailers and professional service providers. And while I'm not suggesting that you don't understand your market or the economics behind staffing extended office hours, I am reminding you that your customers have changed. Their expectations—our expectations—have changed.

If you don't offer extended hours, they will find others that do. If you aren't available on the weekends, someone else will be.

You can take away blankets on your airline, but people will be cold for hours and remember that they were cold . . . on your airline . . . for hours.

"You don't have any blankets? Please. Not even for money? Not even just one extra blankey?"

"Nope. Sorry."

Are you? Really?

Now, here is the tricky part. There are requests/demands that used to be unheard of but are seeming less unreasonable each year. They don't always make sense economically, but they are out there:

Do you offer free delivery? More and more are providing it.

How about free shipping? The big players offer it.

Same-day service? Those who do the work locally can.

Once again, there may not be an economically feasible way to compete with the big players on this issue. Just know that this is a looming challenge for many industries. If Amazon can succeed with low margins and high volume—and throw in free shipping—how are the rest of us supposed to survive? That, my friends, is not a rhetorical question. We have to find the answer. We have to find a way.

If there are items or services that you simply cannot afford to provide, then you have to back-fill with something else of value for your prospects to stay in the game. I'm not suggesting that you have to provide everything your prospects want, and at the price they want, but you do have to take your competitors' offerings into account. They are an attractive alternative to you and are aggressively competing for your customers. They can't be ignored. So what can you offer?

Your customers will not only notice what you don't offer, they will remember it, often fume over it, and likely tell others. Think long and hard about every time you or your staff say no. Better yet, have them make notations of every request they say no to. Remember, you are not your customers. Don't rely on what is important to you. Ask yourself and notice what is important to them. If they are asking for something on a regular basis, find a way to provide it or a reasonable alternative. Often, simply recovering the lost revenue from those you drive away is sufficient to fund offering the desired item or service.

I was looking for a restaurant where I could meet with a colleague. I wasn't sure if the one I was interested in was open for lunch, and I couldn't find any hours listed on their website. So I simply moved on to another restaurant that made it easy for me to find out what their hours were.

Everything else can be fine, but we will notice what you don't have. For example:

No bedside power outlets in hotel rooms. (Uh, its 2019. Spend a dollar and update your room.)

No baby-changing station. (A bigger problem in the men's room.)

No hook for your suit jacket in the bathroom stall. (Businessmen are out of luck.)

No toilet paper left in your restroom. (Someone needs to be in charge of this. It's not an afterthought.)

No free delivery (or any delivery) within a local area. (If others offer it, you are at a competitive disadvantage.)

Bathrooms without air freshener. (People appreciate that you thought of this!)

Napkins behind the counter. (Why do we have to ask for napkins? Put them on the table, for crying out loud.)

Not accepting credit cards. (Let me just write this on a stone tablet.)

No hot water in the sink in the bathroom. (Are the employees washing with cold water too? 'Nuff said.)

Not enough parking. (Make arrangements to supplement. You are losing customers left and right if they know parking will be a hassle.)

A twenty-four-hour contact option. (Open for regular business hours. So that means you are closed for sixteen out of twenty-four hours a day and all weekend. Hmm.)

Weekend hours. (See above.)

Next-day shipping. (Yes, we are spoiled. Sure, but we have money. Do you want it or not?)

WHY YOU DO IT:

Most of the things you don't offer are related to your original business model. This is how we have done business, and these are the amenities and services we offer. Most of what people demand today are part of the new dynamic. Wi-Fi didn't exist when our building was built. We didn't need so many electrical outlets ten years ago. The challenge comes from clinging to the founder's mindset when your cheese is being moved and eaten by competitors.

WHY WE HATE IT:

The world has changed and our expectations with it. We take your lack of foresight, insight, or responsiveness as a personal slight. Others care about amenities, but you clearly don't. And if you don't care about us, we don't care about you.

A BETTER APPROACH:

Listen to your customers. They are telling you what they want and what they expect from those they buy from. You don't alway have to say yes, but you are going to have to say it more often in the months and years to come. You can stand on principle, or you can ring up orders. You can reject the expenditure, or you can invest to ensure a viable ongoing business proposition. It's going to take bold thinking and flexibility on your part. It's not about what you want to sell, it's what they want to buy.

Here is a question: What is worth more, fifty dollars earned from selling something that your customers have loved for decades, or fifty dollars from offering a new item that would have made the company's founder roll over in his grave? You already know the answer.

18

Your Management Fails to Manage

Do every job you're in like you're going to do it for the rest
of your life, and demonstrate that ownership of it.
–Mary Barra, CEO of General Motors

❝These damn kids don't want to work. They come in late and think that I should chill out! They text on their phones when they should be helping customers, and if you try to call them out, they say, 'Screw this, I'm out of here.' What are you supposed to do?"

I'll tell you what you're supposed to do: Do your job. Manage your employees. If a bad employee leaves because they're being held accountable for their job responsibilities, good! You didn't need them anyway. Don't tell me that a warm body is better than nothing. It's not. A recently deceased corpse is a warm body. Your customers and clients deserve better—and not just from them—from you!

Poor customer service is really a reflection of managers failing to hold their people accountable to provide strong service. Employees with attitudes, texting, socializing, and not being held accountable for strong work and good service is not a customer service issue. It's a leadership issue.

Weak leaders are either lazy, clueless, or fearful. They just don't care, so their employees won't either; or they are afraid of coming down on their people for fear of losing them; or they simply lack the leadership skills necessary to be an effective manager. If any of this resonates with you or applies to your leadership team, then I promise you are losing customers.

Regardless of the reason, if leaders don't mandate the delivery of strong service, it simply won't happen. And when service and respect wanes, your customers will leave for better options—in droves. Once again, because they can.

You've heard the old maxim "What you tolerate, you encourage." When service is spotty, that is bad enough, but when the bar consistently is set low, that's the fault of management. Lest you think that raising the bar will cause a mutiny or heightened employee dissatisfaction, studies have clearly show that organizations with the highest expectation in terms of service and behavior have the happiest employees. Because, of course, providing great service creates not only happy customers, but also happy employees as well. Everyone is happier and so they treat each other better. It's not rocket surgery!

There is a famous scene in the movie *Big* where Tom Hanks's character begins working as an adult in an office. As he sits and begins to crank away, a guy in the adjacent cubicle (Jon Lovitz) urges him to slow down because if he is overly productive, then everyone will have to work harder. The culture dictates the level of performance, and the culture is created and fostered from the top down. This is the same dynamic that occurs in any workplace where underperformance or a lackadaisical attitude is the norm. It becomes the prevailing culture, and any new employee is slowly absorbed into the malaise.

Conversely, when the bar is set high, expectations are clear, and there is little tolerance for poor service or underperformance as the slackers tend to stand out. The poor performers are looked down upon, and the prevailing excellence actually becomes the catalyst for conformity. Everyone cares for the customers because "that's what we do."

We often see some of the poorest service in businesses whose customers are a bit transient. If it's likely a one-time purchase, where is the incentive to build goodwill? Airport restaurants are notorious for poor service. Some waitstaff will work hard for the tip, but others clearly care less because "we'll never see these guys again."

I was at a chain restaurant at Chicago's O'Hare airport and found myself in the middle of a reasonably long line to be seated. There were a multitude of empty tables, though most of them were dirty. The problem from the line's perspective, was that the line was not moving. The hostess walked by—slowly—again and again, without acknowledging the people waiting. Being the extrovert that I am, I called over from my place, fifth in line, and said, "Excuse me. Can we be seated?"

She shot her head around, glared at the line, and said with attitude, "When it's your turn!"

The first person in line asked sheepishly, "Can it be my turn?"

The hostess grabbed a handful of menus, turned her back, and walked into the restaurant. The couple in the front turned to the others in line and asked, "Should we follow her?"

Inside the restaurant was not much better. Every person seemed either really busy or lazy and nonchalant. None provided even a reasonable level of service. I had no idea who the manager was or who was in charge. What was clear, was that no one was holding anyone accountable. As much as I wanted to be angry with the indifferent staff members, they wouldn't have cared anyway. I was traveling through Chicago on the way to Denver, and they would never see me again. And if their manager didn't care, why should they? It was clear that they were correct on both counts.

My intent is not to trash a business but to remind you that we notice. We care. We watch, and we share. I'm not telling a dozen of my friends. I'm telling the thousands (perhaps hundreds of thousands) who are reading this.

The strategy for pervasive underperformance and spotty service? Leadership, modeling, mentorship, management, and diligence (LMMMD).

Leadership: It is up to you to take the initiative to get this under control and create a program. Weak leaders avoid uncomfortable confrontation. Strong leaders take the issue head on and set the standard for their people. They will look to you and you have to come through.

Modeling: You have to be in the trenches modeling the behavior that you expect of your people. They will notice your deeds as much as your words.

Mentorship: People are not born with these skill sets. You inherit the attitude brought by your people, but you can teach the skills they need to know. Teach, model, and mentor.

Management: Nothing good will happen without management, oversight, and accountability. When you are not there, someone has to be in charge, not merely of the business transactions and back office, but of the people as well!

Diligence: Substitute the word "consistency" if you want. Regardless, this is not about the hoopla of the launch. This is every day, every interaction, every scenario—today, tomorrow, and every day. You have to be relentless in your expectations and stay on top of it. Your customers will notice when you slack off or become inconsistent.

Just as we tell our own teens when they get their driver's license to assume that everyone on the road is trying to kill you, you have to assume that every customer is looking for an excuse to leave you. Don't let your employees hand them that excuse.

I learned an important lesson a quarter century ago when I sang with an a cappella group called The Diners. We were pretty darned good and were booked to play nightclubs on a regular basis and a slew of private parties and other events.

One summer, we were hired to perform at a very swanky wedding at an upscale ski resort in Beaver Creek, Colorado. The family had spent a good chunk of change for the reception that was held in a gigantic white tent at the base of a mountain. We were positioned on a small stage at one end inside the tent and had a full sound system with microphones, stands, and other equipment. The dinner tables filled most of the floor area, and there was a dance floor between us.

As is often true at events like this, we were certainly not the focus of the event. We were background music, and while some danced, most ate and socialized throughout the big tent.

As we performed, took requests, and played our role as the background music, we admittedly started screwing around a little too much. We got the giggles from inside jokes, maybe changed a lyric here and there to get one of the guys laughing, and generally decided to have a good time whether anyone was listening or not.

Between songs, an older gentleman in a nice tuxedo approached us, I assumed to request a song. But as I leaned down from the edge of the stage, he positioned himself next to my left ear, and in a very calm but direct voice, he said something that has resonated with me to this day.

"Two things," he said. "Remember that someone is always watching, and you are being paid for this."

With that, he backed away, locked eyes with me, and raised an eyebrow as he turned to rejoin the wedding party. I wanted to throw up. He was right. Dead right. I gathered the guys in a quick huddle and relayed the man's words. It changed everything about the next two hours—and likely for the years that followed.

That lesson has stuck with me for decades and rings even truer in this age of social media. Not only is everyone watching, everyone is recording and reporting. You have to assume that bad behavior in your business is being noticed, noted, and shared. This is true for everyone on your team—every interaction and transaction.

One clear problem in terms of providing and managing strong service is the lack of clarity and specificity of what is expected. Attitude plays a large role, but it's the specific be-haviors that must be taught, reinforced, and expected.

"Every guest must be treated like family" is a bit amor-phous. We treat family members differently—some better than others. I know people who treaty their family like crap. A better approach is:

"Every guest is to be greeted with eye contact and a smile. Everyone, every time. If you are walking toward a guest, you will be the first to acknowledge and greet them. Here are the exact words we use to greet people on the phone, at the front desk, at the register, and so on."

When they know the performance standard in your business, and the application is consistent from leadership, people will conform. They rise to the level of your expecta-tion. And to reasonably expect your people to know the ser-vice standard they are expected to deliver, you must provide it to them, train them on it, reinforce it, revisit it, and hold them accountable.

Here is the uncomfortable truth: If you boast about your great customer service, but don't have a specific training program to train your people on what you expect, if you are not evaluating your people based on their customer service delivery, if you are not compensating them based on their meeting the standard you have set, then you have no right to claim it! Why? Because you have no way of ensuring its consistent delivery! It's just blah, blah, blah.

The other question is: Who is responsible for ensuring compliance and excellence when you are not around? It's not a surprise that employee theft in small businesses increases exponentially when the boss isn't around. Bartenders over-pour and give away drinks, merchandise is missing, and slacking in general increases significantly when the boss is away. Achieving a consistently strong service culture is directly proportionate to the active presence of leadership during working hours. If you aren't there and in charge, someone has to be.

WHY YOU DO IT:

Managing is hard. Okay. And? You are in business, and despite what you hate about the people part of it, it is incumbent upon you to step up and do the hard part of your job: hold people accountable for the jobs they are being paid to do. They are not seat warmers. They are not clock watchers. They are brand ambassadors. If your leaders are reluctant to hold those they manage accountable, then they need to be trained, moved, or fired. Groom or broom, as they say.

WHY WE HATE IT:

Everyone hates poor service, but we hate it more when our concerns fall on deaf ears. Someone has to be accountable for the team, and when management isn't, everything falls apart—and we fall hard for that attractive competitor of yours.

A BETTER APPROACH:

Your leaders need to be evaluated and compensated based on the performance of their team. Train them, equip them, empower them, reward them, and make sure they have all the tools they need to succeed. If you are that leader, step up, friend. Find the motivation from wherever you need, but step up and be the leader your team and your customers need you to be. The good news is that when you do, everyone (except the people who need to go) wins.

19

SHOW US THAT YOU CARE
ABOUT YOUR BUSINESS

The queen thinks the world smells of fresh paint.
–British saying

At the most basic and primal level, we avoid situations that feel uncomfortable. In Malcolm Gladwell's groundbreaking and enlightening book *Blink: The Power of Thinking Without Thinking,* he wrote of the unconscious factors that affect our perception of situations, environments, and locations. When something doesn't feel quite right, it is likely a function of our mind processing factors that are beyond our conscious comprehension. It's the minutia, the little things, that can alter our perception.

A dark alley or a cold, musty business feels like somewhere that might be populated by shady characters or where you might get assaulted. Old phones generate feelings of nostalgia. The smell of burning grease reminds us of a dirty street vendor or a bad breakfast in our youth. Everything we experience through our senses is filtered through our view of the world and our previous experiences and memories.

The same feelings come into play when you fail to provide a clean, safe, uncluttered, conducive environment for us to work, shop, or buy. We connect your lack of efficiency or questionable maintenance with negative feelings and emotions. There is a big difference between nostalgic and old; rustic and poorly maintained.

When we see your dirty bathrooms, we know something important about you, your mentality, your work ethic, your leadership style, and your priorities. When there are rips in your seating, layers of dust on the ceiling fan, and burned out light bulbs, we wonder what else have you stopped paying attention to. When the magazines in your waiting room are from the first Bush administration, we know that things are being missed.

Many of these dynamics play out on the television business turnaround shows like *The Profit* or *Bar Rescue*. Often, before he will even consider putting money into a tavern, *Bar Rescue* host John Taffer will rake the owner over the coals for the bar's pathetic lack of basic cleanliness or maintenance. That alone is often the biggest predictor of customers fleeing the location in droves. It's clear that the owner stopped caring, and if the owner doesn't care, the employees sure as hell aren't going to care!

So, what message does this send to customers, clients, and prospects, and does it really have an impact? Let's look at it from two perspectives: The safe choice perspective and the competitive marketplace one.

One school of thought asserts that there is a mistaken belief that everyone is looking to make the best decision possible when it comes to purchasing, hiring, and contracting. Of course, we would like to always make the best decision, but the problem is that we don't know what that is because everyone tells us that they're great. The reality is that we are really looking to avoid making a bad decision. We don't want to screw it up.

We know what a day of downtime, a bad meal, failed installation, late delivery, or poor service would cost our business. We don't want to take a chance. With all the choices in front of us, provided they are priced competitively, we opt for the safe choice.

Of course, "safe" is relative depending on the industry. If we are looking for a financial planner, a little grey hair shows age and experience, and that can help us feel pretty safe. That candidate has been around the block a few times.

The general contractor who has been in business for a hundred years and built a third of the local skyline is safe. However, the oldest technology company isn't safe. We don't gravitate toward the company that boasts, "We've been making slide projectors since Hewlett met Packard on the playground in third grade." An old contractor is safe, but an old technology company is not.

Do you know what else is not safe? A poorly maintained retail store, office, parking lot, bathroom, or even website. What feels unsafe is burned out light bulbs, disorganized warehouse shelves, voicemail with a message notifying of a holiday closing two months prior, or a hotel room with mold in the corner of the shower.

When you don't care enough to hold your people accountable for daily cleaning and scheduled maintenance, we notice. When you haven't invested in current technology for your staff or art for your walls, we assume that you are not making any money—because you must not be very good. Translation: You are not a safe choice.

The other reason is more basic and far more prevalent: It's a competitive marketplace, and we don't choose tired, outdated businesses because we don't have to. In yesteryear, the choice was to accept a company that was less than ideal or take the time to drive across town for something better. Too often, we opted for the convenience of the choice that was closest to home, despite their deficiencies.

We rarely face that dilemma anymore. Choices are everywhere! Often, another choice is merely a click, call, or email away. We choose other businesses that are more contemporary, clean, functional, streamlined, and current, simply because we can easily do so.

When you are enjoying a meal at a good restaurant but find the restroom disgusting (pretty standard for the men's restroom), it taints your entire view of the experience, from the food to the service and more.

If you walk into a dentist's office and the waiting room cushions are ripped and the ceiling tiles have water stains, you would question the sterility and the safety of the procedures.

If you look up a marketing firm online, and their website has a Flash animation video on a landing page that explains their business before you get to their home page, like companies had ten years ago that everyone clicked to skip, you would question how current they were.

And if you walk into a consulting firm and everyone is dressed five steps below Casual Friday, you might question their professionalism and how seriously they took their business.

When it comes to your prospective customers' first and lasting impression of you, everything matters. We all judge books by their covers. We make snap judgments and move forward with preconceived ideas. If you feed into our fears, you will struggle to even get up to bat.

Listen, there are enough reasons to choose others without handing customers additional excuses. Unfortunately, taking care of your business and keeping it clean and current isn't going to create any competitive advantages, unless your industry is notorious for it's tired, worn appearance. It will merely put you on par with others who are taking care of their business. But at least you won't be behind the eight ball.

WHY YOU DO IT:

You don't pay attention to the details too often because you are paying attention to the big picture. Then again, you might just be cheap and simply holding off on updating your decor because you don't want to spent the money.

Your place is dirty because you are reluctant to hold your people accountable for jobs they should be doing. You either want to be liked or you are afraid of confrontation or pushback from people who assert that it isn't their job to clean or maintain. Whatever the reason, get over it. You are driving customers away because you are failing to maintain or upgrade your location or website.

WHY WE HATE IT:

Why should we care about you and your business if you don't? When your business looks tired or outdated, we look elsewhere. When you smell bad, we turn up our nose. When you are falling apart, we fall into the arms of another.

A BETTER APPROACH:

Do a little informal market research. Secret shop your competitors to get a good sense of their decor. Visit their website and gauge yourself against them. Your prospects are already doing this. You need to know what they see.

Now, do an honest audit of your business. Walk through with fresh eyes, and ask a trusted colleague (who does not work for you) to accompany you on this journey of self-discovery.

Make a comprehensive list of everything that does not look great, clean, and fresh. Be honest, and be hard on yourself. Then, go through and prioritize the refresh, replacement, or remodeling. Every item gets a date, even if it's a year away or further. You may not be able to correct everything right away, but you need to have a plan for everything to get done. First things first: clean!

20

STOP WASTING OUR TIME

Remember that no one will share your sense of urgency.
–Philip Avrin

I f there is an issue that has become the primary driver of our decisions in recent years, it's time. It's not just that we hate to wait (we do), it is that we often struggle to get done what we have to do in the time we have.

We constantly dart back and forth on the highway looking for the faster-moving lane—even if it buys us only a few seconds on our journey. We get frustrated waiting for websites to load, traffic lights to turn green, and the microwave to pop our popcorn.

And if there is anything we hate more than waiting, it's wasting time. The word "wasting" has a connotation that the wait was unnecessary. It was through incompetence, poor planning, or poor policies that we are forced to waste our time waiting for you.

Why have we accepted the fact that medical professionals will often see an appointment as a mere suggestion and not an agreement? We are expected to arrive on time, but they will see us when they get to us. To placate us, we are led into the exam room to wait some more. Of course, they might be caught up with a serious medical case, but shouldn't they plan for that and leave a cushion? It's not like they don't have a good sense of what an average day looks like.

Perhaps we have a lunch appointment time and the other person arrives twenty minutes late, out of breath and exasperated. "So sorry. Traffic was crazy!" he says while throwing his coat on the seat, flopping into the restaurant booth, and opening the menu.

"Really?" I think to myself. "I made it on time. I figured there would be traffic at lunch time and left a little early." Now, the tone has changed. Someone feels disrespected and the goodwill that had been built up to that point has been damaged. It's not that things don't come up. Of course they do. But are you really doing everything you can to respect the time of your customers and prospects?

For decades, car dealers had perfected the "full day at the dealership." Why does it take so darn long to buy a car? When we think we have a selection in mind, the salesman disappears to talk to the sales manager to try and "work the numbers." Of course, the only numbers being discussed were the football scores from Sunday's games or the number of fish they were going to catch on next week's camping trip.

The dynamic, which has been long studied, dictated that the longer a car dealership kept you on the lot, the less likely you would leave, feeling that you had invested so much time in this deal that you wouldn't want to start over at another dealership. Time was on their side. No longer.

We don't merely want what we want, when we want it (we do), we also want answers when we want them. We want resolution to our problems—not next week, not when So-and-So is back in town. We want it now. Don't waste my time with excuses. Don't waste my time trying to placate me. Get me someone with the authority to solve my problem and give me the answer I am looking for—even if it's not the answer I want! Just stop wasting my time.

There is an interesting dichotomy at work: Of course, we want the resolution we are looking for, and we don't want excuses. We want you to tell us that we can have what we want. That's a given. But if there are times where we won't get what we want because there just isn't the structure to supply it, or there isn't time to get it to our destination, just don't make us find out after having lost three days waiting. Get to the answer, get us to a manager or someone with authority— now. Don't waste our time. We aren't always going to win. We know that. We won't be happy, but we can accept that. What we can't accept is wasting a day to get to that point.

It's the same frustrating feeling we get when our computer crashes and we lose the report, document, term paper, or book chapter that we failed to back up. Arrrrghh! Not only did we lose all of our work, we will lose five or six hours more redoing it! It's not just frustrating; it's physically painful.

There are a lot of things we can get back in our lives. We can earn back money. We can rekindle a friendship. We can even clear our name and get back our reputation on occasion.

What we can never get back is time. Losing it is one thing. Wasting it is another. We can choose to waste it by vegging out watching TV or playing on social media, but that is *our* choice. You do not have permission to waste our time. Businesses that waste our time lose our business.

If there is a long line for lunch, we will probably go somewhere else. If we are told that hold times are approaching forty minutes, we hang up. We get impatient sitting at a thirty-second red light, so why do you think we will patiently wait for you to get back to us? Worse yet, is if we feel that the wait is unnecessary and simply a function of your understaffing or moving like molasses. The only times we are willing wait is if we want to. Waiting for a bay at TopGolf is worth it!

We are also willing to wait at the Department of Motor Vehicles because there is no choice. Do we want to drive or not? It's a "have to." But if it's a "get to," we will probably leave.

Today, we actively seek expedited options. Carvana says that you can "buy the car, without the car salesman." Amazon is starting to offer same-day delivery in some cities. What do you offer or provide that makes better use of your customer's time? What do you do to get them in and out or on their way faster? Customers value their time. Do you?

WHY YOU DO IT:

Time is relative. What we think is reasonable may look like molasses to someone in a hurry. Remember that your job is not merely to manage the delivery of your goods and services. It's not simply about what is reasonable and efficient. The meaningful perception emanates from your customer or prospect. What does fast look like to them? What is a reasonable wait time from their perspective?

WHY WE HATE IT:

There is always something we'd rather be doing something we don't want to be doing. The less time we spend on things we don't enjoy, the better. If we know that our time was wasted unnecessarily, then we hold that person or business responsible. The punishment? The loss of our business.

A BETTER APPROACH:

Don't merely gauge your efficiency and effectiveness based on internal standards. Don't look at your delivery based solely on whether or not the transaction was complete, the sale went through, or the product was delivered. Look at every point along your customer's journey and ask if each interaction went as it should have. Could it have been smoother, faster, more transparent, better shepherded, more tailored, or more personalized?

The customers get to decide whether they feel their time was respected or wasted. We have great influence on which way that needle is going to fall. The solution is to move upstream and design a customer journey (and the corresponding behaviors) that are designed to expedite and enhance their interactions with us.

21

STOP BEING CHEAP

*What we obtain too cheap, we esteem too lightly; it
is dearness only that gives everything its value.*
–Thomas Paine

Efficiency is reasonable. Smart spending is understand-
able. Cheap is just cheap. Scraping chunks of dripped
toothpaste off the bathroom counter and using them as
after-dinner mints is cheap. Making us request napkins or
soy sauce that you keep behind the counter, and then asking
how many we want, is cheap.

Like the creepy neighbor who stands on his driveway on
Halloween handing out pennies pulled from his jacket pocket,
we have disdain for those who skimp on basic amenities and
intentionally give us less than we want, less then we feel we
deserve.

A well-known leadership organization had been recently purchased by a private equity company and was looking for ways to cut expenses to increase the bottom line. In addition to exploring operational efficiencies, they were also looking at the minutiae to achieve real dollar savings. (Smart move, as you can often derive dollars from the details.) But anytime you cut (or gut) customer-facing services or amenities, you are treading on dangerous ground.

One of the items under serious consideration was eliminating the plaques given to members who had participated in the program for five years, ten years, and so on. Now, understand that these members were paying nearly $15,000 per year for in-depth business-building sessions with their CEO peers. Every few months, on special anniversary days, they would take a few minutes away of the agenda to pause and honor those companies leaders who have been members of the group for many years. It was proposed that the plaques be eliminated to save money. (By the way, the plaques cost around twenty dollars.)

Really? This is what you want to cut? A twenty-dollar plaque for a company leader who has invested six figures with your organization? The pushback was swift, and these very reasonable tokens of appreciation remained.

"Can I get some ketchup, please?" you say to the person at the drive-thru window after checking your bag and finding none. I mean, there are two large orders of french fries and three burgers in the bag. Don't they generally throw ketchup in the bag?

"How many do you want?" he asks.

"Oh, I don't know. Five?" you stammer.

He counts out exactly five ketchup packets, lips moving as he counts, and hands them to you.

"Can you tell me where the napkins are?" you ask the lady at the takeout register. She reaches to her stack, out of your reach, and hands you one napkin.

Are we not adults? Can we not determine for ourselves how many napkins we need to wipe our faces and hands after eating the meal that we just purchased? Cheap. A minor issue? Yes. But an unnecessary annoyance. Dumb.

Your customers notice when you are cheap. We notice when the plastic fork is flimsy, the check-in counter is understaffed, the portion sizes are too small, and the packaging is deceptive for the amount of actual product contained inside. You look cheap, and we feel cheated.

It is wise in business to review every expenditure and seek ways to reduce cost and increase efficiency. There are financial experts that could go into any organization and help them decrease costs by 5 percent to 10 percent in less than a week. Easy peasy. However, because my professional work and mindset is on the revenue-generating side of the ledger, I would rail against most of those cuts.

Cutting costs is not difficult. Reducing unnecessary expenditures without an adverse effect on sales or customer retention is difficult. On paper, you could easily fire people, eliminate services, reduce amenities, and cancel previously enjoyed benefits. What would you have left?

This is a wake-up call. The entire book is about conscious, strategic decisions that companies make that effect their level of service, availability, comfort, effectiveness, speed, and preferability. Far too many companies are choosing poorly. They are managing rather than serving. They are restricting rather than delivering. Decisions too often are being made by MBAs and bookkeepers, rather than in concert with sales and customer experience managers.

Amazon CEO Jeff Bezos is famous for his "Day 1" philosophy and mindset. That mindset was not about managing a business, but maintaining a sense of urgency. Each year, he republishes the 1997 letter he sent to shareholders of his new company on their first day. Here is an excerpt:

This is Day 1 for the Internet and, if we execute well, for Amazon. Today, online commerce saves customers money and precious time. Tomorrow, through personalization, online commerce will accelerate the very process of discovery. Amazon uses the Internet to create real value for its customers and, by doing so, hopes to create an enduring franchise, even in established and large markets.

Though we are optimistic, we must remain vigilant and maintain a sense of urgency. The challenges and hurdles we will face to make our long-term vision for Amazon a reality are several: aggressive, capable, well-funded competition; considerable growth challenges and execution risk; the risks of product and geographic expansion; and the need for large continuing investments to meet an expanding market opportunity.

Jeff Bezos reminds his team that it is always Day 1. The mindset is not about managing, but growing. It's not merely about efficiency, but about pushing the boundaries and always getting better. They don't circle the wagons; they send them out to look for new opportunities.

Years later, Bezos was asked what Day 2 looks like. His response: "Day 2 is stasis. Followed by irrelevance. Followed by excruciating, painful decline. Followed by death. And that is why it is always Day 1."

When you are cheap with your customers, it's Day 2.

WHY YOU DO IT:

Companies confuse "frugal" with "cheap" because they are blind to, or refuse to see, the implications. I don't think most in business set out to be unkind, but when you deny the use of your restrooms unless someone pays you for something, you come across as mean and petty. You are cheap because it saves you money. Unfortunately, you may be paying a hefty price for what you consider frugal. We notice. We recoil and we share—not just your cheap behavior, but our reduced opinion of you. Was the penny for every ten napkins worth it?

WHY WE HATE IT:

Our perception of value received for dollars spent is directly tied to whether or not we will repeat that experience. If the meal costs twenty-four dollars and we equate the quality to a fast-causal alternative that would have cost half that amount, we aren't likely to return. If we buy a jacket and the materials and craftsmanship feel cheap, we will return the garment or simply never return to the merchant. "Cheap" is not a term you want connected to your business.

A BETTER APPROACH:

Take the blinders off. Walk through your customers' journey with fresh eyes. Look at everything they see, touch, interact with, and take with them. If some part of their experience nullifies all the good that you do, then address it. If something lowers their perception of your quality or commitment to your business, be willing to pay a little more to address it. Just as cost-cutting requires a conscious decision, so too does excellence. Which do you think your customers are looking for?

Don't Take Us for Granted

Life is a matter of courtship and wooing, flirting and chatting.
–Carolyn See

G rowing up in the 1960s, I remember going to the bank with my father and seeing a small display featuring a shiny new toaster. I asked my dad if they were making toast for the bank customers. He just laughed and said that the toaster was a premium for opening a new account.

"What's a premium?" I asked.

"It's like a prize or gift that they offer for new customers," he responded.

"Do we get a new toaster?" I inquired.

"No," he said brushing off the question. "That's just for new customers."

"So, what do we get," I pressed.

"Uh, nothing, I guess. You get a lollipop!" he smiled as he walked up to the bank teller.

We spend a lot of time in business chasing new customers and clients. We have to keep the pipeline full, and if we want to be in business next year, we can never stop marketing. My question is: Besides delivering what is expected of you, what are you doing to keep your current customers happy and feeling valued?

Many a marriage will fail when the partners stop wooing each other and take each other for granted. Life gets in the way, kids are demanding, and date nights become all the more infrequent. The next thing you know, the partner that you promised to love, honor, and cherish is feeling ignored, resentful, and taken for granted. Where did it go wrong?

It is a common dynamic in business as well. We work hard to impress new prospects. We put our best foot forward and show them extra time and attention. Our early work with them is top notch. We communicate often and check in to make sure everything is on track.

Then, inevitably, we start to get a little too comfortable—perhaps even a bit cocky. "Oh, they love us. They've been with us forever!" we think dismissively. They might be regulars at our restaurant or long-time clients of our firm. We are the vendor of choice or the familiar retail destination. It's not that we stop doing a good job or stop working hard, we just stop doing the extras or finding ways to improve the experience. We're too comfortable and way too confident.

Our biggest threat with long-time customers or clients is complacency. The persistent challenge to your business comes from competitors who would love to treat our long-time customer like their first-time customer. They want to wine and dine, woo and cajole them, make them feel like a queen or king. Who do you think is working harder to impress your long-time customers, you or the company that wants to replace you?

Data from the Gartner Group showed that 68 percent of customers leave because they perceive that you are indifferent to them.[1]

Don't be lulled into thinking that your loyal customers will remain loyal simply because you do a good job for them. Without time, attention, and connection along with consistent, appreciative engagement, your client's eyes will wander. They will see the perks and incentives offered by others for new customers, and they will be tempted! You don't get to keep your customers merely because you earned them and serve them.

I was leaving a hotel one afternoon and was directed by the bellman to a line of taxis waiting outside. As the bellman was loading my bags into the trunk, I leaned in the passenger side window to talk to the taxi driver, and I asked if he accepted American Express. He didn't look at me or respond.

"Excuse me. Is this just a cash-only cab, or do you accept American Express?" I repeated.

Once again, he didn't look at me, but took his right hand off the wheel and made a kind of a small "whatever" motion.

With that, I yelled over to the bellman who was walking away, "Take my bags out of the trunk!" I walked to the next taxi in line.

The taxi driver threw open his door and rushed around the back, shouting: "What? Wait! No!" and tried to take the bags back from the bellman."

I shouted over to him, "I asked you the same question twice, and not only would you not answer, but you wouldn't even look at me! You assumed I had to do business with you because you were next in line. I don't. You lost the right to my business. You treated me poorly. I would have treated you even better and given you a big tip, but now you get to wait for the next person."

I apologized to the bellman who nodded and said, "No. Wow! I agree with everything you said!"

I shouted to the next taxi driver in line who was standing by his car listening to the exchange: "Do you take American Express?"

"Absolutely!" He responded with a smile as the bellman loaded my luggage in his car.

The lesson is that you can't assume and expect that any-one will do business with you because they are supposed to. Whether you have been doing business with them for an extended period, you are the closest option, or simply the next one in line, customers always have choices. Give them a good reason to want to do business, keep working to earn their business even if you already have their business, and they'll keep doing business with you.

When other things are more important to your employees than we are, we feel like you don't care. When they are talking on their cell phones, we feel reluctant to interrupt. When your employees are gossiping in front of us, or complaining about coworkers or other customers, we feel uncomfortable.

Just because we've done business with you before doesn't mean that you have to stop trying. A much repeated maxim reminds us that "Every company is fired on the last day of each month and hired on the first day of the next one." Every time we write that check, allow that auto payment to go through, or walk into your restaurant, we are judging you with fresh eyes and asking ourselves if we want to continue this relationship. It's not that loyalty is dead. It's just much harder to earn and keep because it is so easy to leave you.

WHY YOU DO IT:

Professionals with a sales mindset are always looking to impress new customers. Of course, we know that it's much cheaper to keep a client happy than to earn a new one, yet we too often focus on new sales at the expense of our loyal customers.

WHY WE HATE IT:

Nobody wants to feel taken for granted. When you used to check in but no longer do, we feel like we're no longer important to you. What am I, chopped liver? (An American colloquialism for my international friends.) When the new customer gets perks that we don't, we wonder how our loyalty is being rewarded.

A BETTER APPROACH:

Check in—often. "How are we doing? Did that last order go smoothly? We are coming to the end of our contract. How can we earn your business for another year?"

Take some time to list all the things you do to woo a new customer or client. What do you offer them? How do you treat them, and how often do you connect? Now, make a list of all your current customers, and discuss how you can offer the same to them as well. Never stop working to show your customers how much they mean to you.

23

Being Good Is No Longer Good Enough

Before you try to keep up with the Joneses, be
sure they're not trying to keep up with you.
–Erma Bombeck

In 1943, Abraham Maslow penned a groundbreaking paper entitled "A Theory of Human Motivation." In it he offered his now famous theory, the Hierarchy of Needs. That list included:

Physiological needs: air, water, food, clothing, shelter, sleep, etc.

Safety: personal, health, financial

Social: love, belonging

Esteem: recognition, respect, importance

Self-actualization: potential, ambition

And while our understanding has grown significantly since that time, Maslow was certainly on the right path.

What is significant is how far we have come as a species to address those basic needs. We have a solution for every problem. It's not to suggest that there not are people in our society who suffer from poverty, hunger, and loneliness. But let's be honest, in the industrialized world, we are pretty darned lucky. Simply put, there are few unmet needs for the vast majority of people. Restaurants dot every block of every major city. We aren't hunting for our food. We push a cart down the aisle of the grocery store or shop online. Few people are sewing their own clothes anymore; we shop at the mall or online.

Put more succinctly, we are spoiled. We live in a time of endless choices and pervasive quality. Most of us no longer have legitimate needs. We have wants. My "need" is a bigger snowblower than Jason has down the street. We are not happy with a roof over our head. We covet that mini-mansion we pass on the way to work. We want Chip and Joanna Gaines to *Fixer Upper* our house (at Waco, Texas, prices!).

We want more than what is good. We want better than good. We want the latest smart phone, the coolest car, and the most coveted basketball shoes. We don't simple want to keep up with the Joneses. We want to be the Joneses!

And with that eye toward the bigger, better deal (BBD), we are always looking for, or at least open to, a better choice. Our eyes are easily turned by shiny objects, and the bigger, better, and cheaper. If you are merely good at what you do, your relationship with your customers is at risk.

When we tout our basic competency, being good at what we do, we leave the door open to those who are better than good. Too often in our marketing, we tout our quality, commitment, caring, trust, customer service, people, freshness, and strong relationships with our current customers. The problem is that those qualities are what we've come to expect from everyone in your space. You'd better have great customer service, or I'm gone. Your food better be fresh, because, well, it's food!

If you are merely good, you are unremarkable. If you meet our needs, we won't trash you online, but we certainly won't rave about you either. I hear company leaders tell their organizations, "Listen, people, at the end of the day, it's about quality!" as the minions nod in approval. I say, "Wrong!" At the *beginning* of the day, it's about quality. Quality is the entry fee. Quality allows you to be in business and open your doors. At the end of the day, it's about competitive advantage.

In this age of options, quality choices are around every corner. I truly believe that the experiences we provide are the differentiators we seek. It is the reason that people come back. It is the reason they leave.

Customer experience may seem like the hot new thing that everyone is talking about—but it's not new at all. Perhaps we have a greater recognition of the importance of a strong experience in this day and age. And perhaps because the Internet tends to "out" underperformers, we are more cognizant of the offenders and lesser players. How we feel about our vendors and service providers has always been the driving force in our decision-making. We do business with people we like, know, and trust.

Your brand promise is who you say you are in the marketplace; your customer experience is how you deliver it. Be intentional. Be strategic. Be wise, but also, be kind. Be empathetic, accommodating, service minded, and humble.

In short, be the kind of company that we want to do business with, and we will continue to do business with you.

My hope is that this book starts a conversation, both inside and outside your company. Conversations lead to recognition and understanding. Understanding leads to action, and actions solve problems. Perhaps we can raise the bar, not just for your business, but for all categories. As they say, "A rising tide lifts all boats." When customer experiences improve, our lives improve, your business improves, and the lives and security of your employees improve along with it.

Oh, and before I forget, can I use your restroom?

AFTERWORD:
BE A GREAT CUSTOMER

Finally, to affect real change in addressing the service deficit, we need to be more than owners, managers, and employees—we need to become advocates. Our biggest role, our biggest impact in the marketplace, is as consumers.

Think about it. We buy more often than we sell, and we visit businesses more often than others visit us. We are all customers, clients, and consumers. And in those roles, we experience the good, the bad, and the ugly when it comes to customer service and broken customer experiences.

What if we took the lessons of this book, the heightened awareness of the prevalence of customer experience shortcomings, and became ambassadors for change? What if we stepped up and became active messengers, calling out poor behavior and flawed policies?

I'm not suggesting unleashing a legion of complainers and malcontents on the world, but of educated, observant messengers intent on affecting positive change. Instead of merely grumbling to friends or posting negative reviews, what if we made a commitment to calling over a manager, motioning to a staffer, or sending a private message to call out poor experiences? Leaders can't address problems they don't know about.

When something goes awry during a restaurant visit, I will make a point to bring it to the attention of my server or a manager. I will say something like, "I just wanted to share with you what I experienced tonight. I am to not looking for a free meal, but as a business owner myself, I know that you can't fix what you don't know about, and I knew that you would appreciate the heads-up." They always appreciate being notified.

While it's important for us to do our part in creating great customer or user experiences in our business, the macro-level change comes from stirring the masses.

One of the goals of the this book is to create more than merely a spark, but a series of brushfires. If I/we can light a fire under the backsides of business owners and leaders, encouraging them to revisit their customer experience journey and ingrained policies, then we can begin to change the expectation on the part of both the customer and the provider.

I harbor no illusions that my little book will create a worldwide revolution of service and enhanced customer experience, but I do hope that it begins thousands of conversations in thousands of organizations. The number of consumers dwarfs the number of business owners. Those of us who play both roles have a special opportunity to have a greater impact—not just in providing great service, but in encouraging it as well.

Notes

Chapter 8

1. Ann Fisher, "U.S. Retail Workers Are No. 1 . . . in Employee Theft," *Forbes,* January 26, 2015. *http://fortune. com/2015/01/26/us-retail-worker-theft/*

2. Elaine Pofeldt, "This Crime in the Workplace Is Costing US Businesses $50 Billion a Year," *CNBC.com,* September 12, 2017. *www.cnbc.com/2017/09/12/workplace-crime-costs-us-businesses-50-billion-a-year.html*

Chapter 10

1. 24/7 Customer, Inc., *2016 Customer Engagement Index,* February 2016.

CHAPTER 12

1. G. Sterling, *Report: Bad Phone Experience Will Send 74 Percent Of Consumers To A Competitor, MarketingLand.com.*

2. Brad Tuttle, "IRS Customer Service Is Even Worse than You Thought," *Money Magazine,* July 16, 2015.

CHAPTER 22

1. *www.retentionofcustomers.com/Customer_Retention_Ideas_Report_Version.htm*

INDEX

accepting work you can't deliver, 20–29

accommodating a customer, the benefits of, 12–13

active listening, the importance of, 118

advertising and email, the evolution of, 31

after hours, allowing customers to reach you, 50

after-hours access, giving customers, 38–45

after-hours purchases, payment options for, 45

agreeing to work
    that you are not qualified for, 23–24
    you can't deliver, 20–29

airlines,
    customer service of, 25–26
    lack of amenities on, 58

always-on business model, 39–40

amenities, providing your customers with, 153

angering a prospect, 85

angry customers, revenue lost from, 113

antiquated websites, 87

appearance of your business, customers and the, 165

ATM, invention and use of the, 39

attitudes, employee, 156

automation, loyalty and, 30–37

automation strategies, misguided, 134

autoresponders, 141, 143

avoiding uncomfortable situations, 164

bad experiences,
    customers and, 91–92
    sharing, 5

bad online reviews, 98

bad reviews, customers and, 96

barriers between your business and your customers, 46

bathroom restriction policies, 14

bias, confirmation, 61

billing department, understaffing your, 49

blame, shifting, 126

brand promise, your, 189–190

business,
    looking for efficiency in your, 138
    outdated appearance of a, 167

business and theft, 75–76

business failure and passion, 100

business hours, reasons for limited, 43–44

business model,
    always-on, 39–40
    focusing on your, 103
    things you don't offer and your, 153

business relationships
  and deceit, 62
  and trust, 62
business values, disingenuous, 58
cash shortages, company losses
  from, 77–78
cheap, the drawbacks of being,
  175–180
checking in with customers, 185–186
clean, keeping your business
  clean, 164–168
client freedom, restricting, 66
clients, your expectations of, 74
closing your business for family
  time, 42
comments, generating positive
  online, 145
communication, efficiency and
  expediting, 31–32
companies that verify personal
  information, 75
company losses, 77–78
company representatives, ways to
  contact, 64–65
company rules, employee
  restraints and, 17–18
competitors, the challenge of,
  182–183
complaints, dissatisfied customers
  and lack of, 97
compliance, leadership and, 161
computer-generated emails to
  customers, 145
confidence, giving your customers,
  112–113
confirmation bias, 61
confusing websites, money lost
  because of, 86–87
connecting with a customer, 116–117
connection,
  four primary ways of, 84–89
  your customers and
  fostering, 119
contact form on your website, 41,
  49, 64, 86
cost-cutting functions, 134
cost savings of eliminating
  gatekeepers, 136
crowd-funded ventures, 107
culture of service, creating a, 122

deceit
  and maximizing profits, 61
  in business relationships, 62
decisions, the importance of
  revisiting past, 71
deflecting problems, 131
delayed responses and customer
  impatience, 51
delivering
  excellence and facilitating a
  transaction, 97
  on your promises, 96
delivery of service, inconsistency
  in the, 123
delivery of services, focusing on, 98
diligence, performance issues
  and, 158–159
direct connection with a prospect,
  the importance of a, 83–84
disingenuous business values, 58
dismissing what customers have
  to say, 66
dissatisfied customers and online
  reviews, 5–6
dissatisfied customers and the
  lack of complaints, 97
e-commerce and Internet
  purchases, 39–40
economy, customers in a
  free-market, 135
effectiveness and efficiency, the
  balance of, 37
efficiency, finding ways to
  increase, 177
efficiency, process flow and, 64
efficiency
  and automation, 31–32
  and effectiveness, the
  balance of, 37
  and your business, 138
email
  addresses, giving out, 144
  and advertising, the
  evolution of, 31
email blasts, 32, 141
  prospects and, 33
  response rates for, 33
email marketing, return on
  investment for, 36
email marketing platforms, uses
  for, 34

emails,
 time savings and mass, 36
 unreturned, 49
employee
 restraints and company
  rules, 17-18
 theft, 77-78
employees,
 different scenarios and
  training your, 20-21
 role-playing with, 126
 staffing, 44
 the physical presence of, 38
estimated wait time, providing
 an, 113
evening hours, extended, 44
expectations of customers and
 clients, your, 74
expedience and responsiveness,
 51-52
expediency and purchase
 decisions, 51
expedited options, customers
 and, 173
expediting communication,
 efficiency, 31-32
expenditures,
 being smart about your, 59
 reviewing, 177
experience, customer, 189
experiences,
 sharing bad, 5
 sharing negative, 5
external workflow, design of the, 64
extracting customer opinions, 145
face-to-face meetings with your
 customers, 84-85
facilitating a transaction and
 delivering excellence, 97
familiar scenarios, training your
 employees for, 20-21
family time, closing your business
 for, 42
flexibility, the benefits of, 16-17
focusing
 on your business model, 103
 on your customers, 103
 on your passion, 102
 on your value proposition, 103
 form letters, 143
franchise model, 19-20
free-market economy, customers
 in a, 135

frequency of purchase, ensuring,
 98-99
frustrated customers, dealing
 with, 119
frustrating a prospect, 85
gatekeepers, cost savings of
 eliminating, 136
generating positive comments
 online, 145
hard-to-find contact information
 on your website, 86
headlines, website, 90
hiring overseas talent, 44-45
hold messages, recorded, 110-111
holding people accountable,
 managers and, 156
homepage, simplifying your,
 82-83
honesty with customers, the
 importance of, 56-57
humanity, 10
immediacy, 9
implementing protectionist
 policies, 75
impressing new prospects, 182
incomplete websites, 87
inconsistency in the delivery of
 service, 123
individuality, 9-10
inflexibility,
 customer frustration and, 20
 saying no and, 16
inflexible policies, the drawbacks
 of, 19
installing verification mechanisms, 81
instant gratification, sacrificing
 your customers for, 142
integrity, the foundation of, 55
interactions, avoiding
 uncomfortable, 126
Internet purchases, e-commerce
 and, 39-40
job satisfaction, process flow and, 64
keeping your business clean,
 164-168
lack of clarity, strong service and,
 160-161
lack of contact information on
 your website, 86
leaders, weak, 156
leaders and mandating strong
 service, 156

leadership, performance issues
    and, 158
leadership
    and compliance, 161
    and performance standards, 161
legal reasons for saying no, 15
limited business hours, reasons
    for, 43–44
live chat feature, 53
location, getting customers to
    come to your, 84–85
logistical reasons for saying no, 15
long-time clients, the biggest
    threat to, 182
lost revenue, biggest source of, 3
lost revenue and email blasts, 33
loyalty,
    accommodation and, 12
    customer, 135
    ways to create, 183
    your customers and fostering, 119
loyalty and automation, 30–37
lying to customers, 56–57
management, performance issues
    and, 158–159
managers and holding people
    accountable, 156
managing for predictability, 19–20
marketing, taking passion out of
    your, 102
marketing
    pitches, bombarding
        customers with, 144
    to previous customers, 146
mass emails, time savings and, 36
mass marketing, lack of response
    to, 35
maximizing profits through deceit, 61
meeting the needs of your
    customers, 96
mentorship, performance issues
    and, 158–159
messages, recorded hold, 110–111
mindset, ownership, 125
minimum viable product, Web
    functionality and, 96
missing goods, company losses
    from, 77–78
mission-driven ventures, 107
modeling, performance issues
    and, 158–159
navigating your organizational
    structure, 136

negative content, reputation
    management and, 6
negative experiences, sharing, 5
negative phone experiences,
    customers and, 112
negative reviews, customers and, 144
no,
    eliminating the word, 20
    hiding behind your policy
        and saying, 16
    inflexibility and saying, 16
    reasons for saying, 15–16
    simple accommodations
        instead of saying, 20
    the power of the word, 11–21
    unfamiliar situations and
        saying, 19
    ways to say, 12
omission, avoiding, 148–154
online experiences, customers
    and poor, 83
online rants, customers and, 96, 144
online reviews,
    bad, 98
    dissatisfied customers and, 5–6
opinions, extracting customer, 145
organizational structure,
    navigating your, 136
original business model, things
    you don't offer and your, 153
outdated appearance of a, 167
overseas talent, hiring 44–45
oversharing, the culture of, 4–5
ownership mindset, 125
passion,
    focusing on your, 102
    marketing and taking out
        your, 102
passion and business failure, 100
passive abdication of responsibility, 125
past decisions, the importance of
    revisiting, 71
payment options for after-hours
    purchases, 45
performance standards and
    leadership, 161
personal information, companies
    that verify, 75
pervasive underperformance, 158
phone, connecting with your
    customers over the, 84–85
phone experiences, customers
    and negative, 112

phone systems, drawbacks of, 110–114
phone-tree systems, 113
physical presence of employees, the, 38
picking up the phone and talking to customers, 48
pitching previous customers, 146
point of contact with customers, looking at the, 97
point-of-purchase tasks, 133
policies,
  inflexible, 19
  replacing strict, 17
policy, saying no and hiding behind your, 16
poor customer service, 156
poor service,
  customers and, 92
  tolerance for, 157
poor word of mouth, 98
positive comments, generating, 145
positive reviews, asking customers for, 145
potential prospects, writing off, 33
PR, the benefits of good, 60
pre-buying behaviors of customers, 85
predictability,
  giving your customers, 112–113
  managing for, 19–20
predictable process flow, benefits of a, 64
preferential reasons for saying, 15
price and purchase decisions, 51
problem-solving, the importance of, 118
problems, deflecting, 131
process flow, benefits of a predictable, 64
processes, customer-centered, 66
profitability, process flow and, 64
promised service, unavailability of a, 26
prospect, directly connecting with a, 83–84
prospects,
  annoyed, 4
  impressing new, 182
  lost revenue and, 3
prospects
  and email blasts, 33

and waiting on your response, 41
protectionist policies, 75
purchase decisions
  and expediency, 51
  and price, 51
purchases, payment options for after-hours, 45
questions, the responsibility of answering customer, 50
recorded hold messages, 110–111
refund policy, 26
relationships, retaining beneficial customer, 137
replacing strict policies, 17
reputation, the importance of your, 8
reputation management and negative content, 6
resolution of issues, delaying, 130
respecting customers' time, 174
response, prospects and waiting on your, 41
response rates for email blasts, 33
response to mass marketing, lack of, 35
responsibility,
  avoiding, 131
  employees who avoid, 130
  passive abdication and, 125
responsiveness and expediency, 51–52
restricting client freedom, 66
restrooms, allowing non-customers to use your, 14
results, delivering authentic, 37
retaining beneficial customer relationships, 137
return on investment for email marketing, 36
revenue lost from angry customers, 113
reviewing expenditures, 177
reviews, dissatisfied customers and online, 5–6
role-playing
  customer scenarios, 123
  with employees, 126
sales specials, bombarding customers with, 144
sales, focusing on, 98
second chances, offering, 91–92
senior staff, rotating, 53–54

service,
        creating a culture of, 122
        inconsistency in the delivery
                of, 123
service delivery, training for the, 116
service empathy, 117–118
service reductions, 133–134
sharing bad experiences, 5
shifting blame, 126
shoplifting, company losses from,
        77–78
social media, contacting customers
        through, 143
socializing, employees and, 156
special requests, accommodating,
        12–13, 17
specificity of what is expected,
        strong service and, 160–161
spin, good PR and, 60
staffing your business with
        employees, 44
streamlined processes, efforts to
        create, 10
stressed customers, dealing with,
        118–122
surge-staffing strategies,
        implementing, 53
surveys,
        bombarding customers with, 144
        customer, 141
talking to customer on the phone, 48
tech support, understaffing your, 49
texting, employees and, 156
thank-you notes, taking the time
        to write, 34
theft,
        businesses and, 75–76
        employees and, 77–78
throwing coworkers under the
        bus, 125–126
time,
        respecting customers', 174
        wasting, 170–174
time savings and mass emails, 36
tolerance for poor service, 157
tracking customer requests, 149
training employees to read your
        customers, 97
transaction, training for the, 116
transparency, the benefits of, 61
trust in business relationships, 62
trusting customers, the
        importance of, 81

unavailability of a promised
        service, 26
uncomfortable interactions,
        avoiding, 126
uncomfortable situations,
        avoiding, 164
underdelivering to customers, 95
underperformance, pervasive, 158
underperformance in the
        workplace, 157
underserved customers, reviews
        from, 24–25
understaffing
        customer service lines, 49
        your billing support, 49
unfamiliar scenarios, training your
        employees for, 20–21
unfamiliar situations, saying no
        in, 19
value proposition, your, 103
values, customers and your, 104–105
verification mechanisms,
        installing, 81
video chat, connecting with
        customers over, 84–85
voicemail, 136
voicemail messages, leaving, 9
wait times, estimated, 113
wasting time, 170–174
weak leaders, 156
web analytics, 83
website,
        customers and your, 84–85
        contact form on your, 49
        fixing a dysfunctional, 82–90
        lack of contact information
                on your, 86
website
        competition, 82
        contact form, 41, 64
        headlines, 90
        page redirection, 85–86
websites,
        antiquated, 87
        cumbersome, 87
        incomplete, 87
        money lost because of
                confusing, 86–87
weekend hours, 44
word of mouth, poor, 98
work performance, process flow
        and, 64
workflow, external, 64

ABOUT THE AUTHOR

David Avrin, CSP, is popular keynote speaker, consultant, and business coach. His marketing and customer experience insights have been featured on hundreds of television news programs and thousands of online and print publications across the globe. As a keynote speaker, David has presented for enthusiastic audiences across North America and in twenty-four countries around the world including Singapore, Bangkok, Melbourne, Barcelona, Rotterdam, Bangalore, Manila, Monte Carlo, London, Buenos Aires, Belfast, Johannesburg, and Dubai.

David Avrin is the president of Visibility International, LLC, offering engaging and entertaining keynote presentations and consulting on marketing and customer experience. Learn more and watch a preview video at *www.VisibilityInternational.com*

He is also the president of The Visibility Coach, offering a select roster of certified small-business marketing experts who provide one-on-one business coaching and resources to small business owners around the world in a low-cost membership model: *www.TheVisibilityCoach.com*

Listen to his podcast: *The VERY Visible Business Podcast* on C-Suite Radio, Apple iTunes, and Stitcher.com.

Check out his blog at: *www.TheVERYVisibleBusiness.blog*

David is also the chief advocate for the 1 Good Turn Campaign, a 501(c)(3) not-for-profit working to lift an entire population of hard-working hotel housekeepers by encouraging travelers to leave a tip when they check out or leave for the day: *www.1GoodTurn.org*

David is the married father of three, the stepfather of two, and lives happily in the south Denver suburb of Castle Rock, Colorado, with his sweetheart, Laurel.

ALSO BY DAVID AVRIN

Business books:

It's Not Who You Know, It's Who Knows You! (Originally published by Wiley, 2009; 2nd edition, Classified Press, 2014)

The 20 Best and Worst Questions Reporters Ask (Classified Press, 2009)

Visibility Marketing (Career Press, 2016)

Sappy books:

The Gift in Every Day—Little Lessons on Living a Big Life (Sourcebooks, 2006)

David Avrin also has stories in three Chicken Soup for the Soul books.

For bulk pricing of any of David's books, contact: info@DavidAvrin.com

Looking for a powerful, high-content, and very entertaining keynote speaker for your next meeting or event? Learn more about David Avrin, CSP, and watch a preview at: www.DavidAvrin.com